WELCOME MEMBERS
TO YOUR
25th ANNUAL
PORK and BEANS
CRAFTSMAN
MW01532409

# People Helping People Since 1945

■ The History of Gascosage Electric Cooperative

# People Helping People Since 1945

■ The History of Gascosage Electric Cooperative

By Pat Swinger

THE
DONNING COMPANY
PUBLISHERS

The Donning Company Publishers
184 Business Park Drive, Suite 206
Virginia Beach, VA 23462

Steve Mull, *General Manager*
Barbara Buchanan, *Office Manager*
Anne Burns, *Editor*
Stephanie Danko, *Graphic Designer*
Priscilla Odango, *Imaging Artist*
Tonya Washam, *Marketing Specialist*
Pamela Engelhard, *Marketing Advisor*

John Richardson, *Project Director*

**Library of Congress Cataloging-in-Publication Data**

Swinger, Patricia, 1951-
People helping people since 1945 : the history of Gascosage Electric Cooperative / by Pat Swinger.
p. cm.
Includes index.
ISBN 978-1-57864-708-8
1. Electric cooperatives—Missouri—History. 2. Electric utilities—Missouri—History. 3. Gascosage Electric Cooperative—History. I. Title.
HD9685.U6M59 2011
334'.6813337932097785—dc23

2011026435

Printed in the United States of America at Walsworth Publishing Company

# Contents

**HUSCH BLACKWELL**

Gascosage Electric Cooperative
Drawer G
Dixon, Missouri 65459

How well I remember the gulf between services that were available to large cities and rural farm communities when I was growing up in Missouri. Gascosage Electric Cooperative is a perfect example of the benefits of joining together and investing in infrastructure that provides for a better life. Cooperatives put us in the position to have modern conveniences and participate in the information age while preserving our rural culture and character. I think that 10,000 members of the Gascosage Electrical Coop would attest that it has been a good investment.

The cooperative concept is what made it possible for us to take our future into our own hands by providing a vehicle to make investments that benefit the community. But, as this book recounts, for cooperatives like Gascosage it become more than a matter of miles of wire and numbers of poles. The idea carried through into community leadership and support. The Coop has been there for its members in good times and bad; it has supported everything from community projects and education programs to aid during natural disasters and hard times.

For these reasons, I was a strong supporter of cooperatives and Gascosage during my years in the Congress and the State Senate. I looked forward to your visits during the Washington Conferences. Your briefings kept me and my colleagues informed of the remarkable progress that coops and their communities made. This book catalogues those impressive results. It is a portion of our history that makes us all proud and I am glad it has been memorialized in this recounting of your history.

Sincerely,

Ike Skelton

Husch Blackwell LLP

# Foreword

■ For almost twenty years it has been both my privilege and my honor to serve as manager of Gascosage Electric Cooperative. Many people have been here longer than myself; some are retired and some are still with us. When I first arrived here from Iowa in 1992, I received a warm and friendly reception and after getting to know everyone, it became clear that this cooperative's greatest asset is the loyal people who work here.

Those of us who grew up in a rural area either remember the days before electricity or we recall listening to our parents and grandparents tell us about how difficult life on the farm was during those years. I don't know if it's really possible for any of us, in this age of microwaves and cell phones, to really appreciate how much work it took just to take care of a family's basic needs back then. But I do know this much: those people who started the rural electric cooperatives following the Great Depression and World War II went to work every day with a sense of mission. The people who lived among the bluffs and valleys of the Gascosage area were their families and friends and every mile of line that was strung, every pole that went up, meant that somebody's life was about to get a whole lot easier.

A lot of things have changed since those early days. Bucket trucks and digger trucks have made new construction a whole lot easier and safer than it was when a lineman's day meant eight hours climbing and working on poles. In the office, computers have replaced hours of posting by hand or on clunky and cumbersome machines. There's no question that our members have become more demanding over the years. Today's rural folks are no longer equipped or accustomed to being without electricity and outages are far more critical for them now than in decades past. One thing is certain—when outages and storms do occur, the people of Gascosage work with the same sense of mission their predecessors had in the early days. They come out all hours of the day or night, in all kinds of weather, over terrain that is no less rocky and no less hilly than it was back then.

This country's rural electric cooperatives, as well as other power providers, will face some challenges in the coming years. I am confident we will work through them, but the questions that lie ahead will best be answered if we remember and appreciate the foundation that was laid for us. We can't forget what it took to bring electricity to the rural people that no one else wanted to invest in, the farmer/directors who helped build a business that gave back to the members, and the men and women of Gascosage Electric Cooperative who made it happen. ■

John Greenlee
*General Manager*

# Acknowledgments

■ We would like to thank the following people who helped us gather the information, photos, and personal anecdotes that went into the production of this book.

Gene Allen
Mike Allen
Karl Brandt
Jim Clark
Bill Davis
John Greenlee
Carmen Hartwell
Somer Overshon
Gayle Prater
Jean Prater
Larry Prater
Norma Riddle
Janet Rigsby
Craig Rivera
Bill Thompson
Walt Weider
James Williams
Pat Williams

# Introduction

■ In 1935, the United States was still in the throes of the Great Depression. Unemployment hovered around 20 percent and millions of Americans were lining up at soup kitchens for their only meal of the day. Approximately 45 percent of America's population lived in rural areas. To help ease the difficult life of the American farmer on whom the entire nation depended for its food supply, Franklin Delano Roosevelt signed legislation forming the Rural Electric Administration in 1935.

Many in Washington, D.C., at the time were skeptical that these farmers possessed the abilities and skills necessary to manage the business of electrifying rural America. To them, we can safely say more than seventy-five years later, the REA has proven to be one of the most successful government programs ever put into place. Indeed, no one was better suited than the American farmer to deal with the challenges of working through rugged terrain, frugally planning for the future, and maintaining optimism while preparing for whatever challenges were ahead.

Gascosage Electric Cooperative was formed in 1945, one of the last cooperatives to be organized in Missouri. Ever since that time, they've been an integral part of the communities they serve, proud of their traditions, optimistic about their future. This history is dedicated to them. ■

Dixon Ice Plant in 1920. Shown are Lester Loveall, engineer, with owners Myrtle and Bennett Skaggs.

CHAPTER ONE

# The Rivers, The Railroad, and Route 66

■ Gascosage Electric Cooperative lies in the Salem Plateau of the Ozark region and takes its name from two rivers that dominate the landscape: the Gasconade and the Osage. While the rivers belong to the area's ancient history, the region's modern history was shaped largely by the coming of the Frisco Railroad and the road that later became known as Route 66.

The drive up Highway 28 to the Dixon office crosses the Gasconade River Valley, exposing ancient bluffs and breathtaking vistas that remain unspoiled and invite one to imagine the first settlers crossing its terrain. Though the first occupants of the area were the Quapaw, Missouria, and Osage Indians, settlers from Kentucky, Tennessee, and the Carolinas stretched their legs and moved westward to the Gascosage area when the War of 1812 treaty brought a relative end to hostilities with the Native Americans. Migrating settlers traveling on land and transporting their household goods and livestock by flatboat may have used the Osage River, a tributary of the Missouri River. The Gasconade, sometimes referred to as "the world's crookedest river," meandered through the plateau creating an abundance of sites for settlement. Since springs abound in the Ozarks, most early settlers used them for drinking, cooking, and washing along the creek banks.

The railroad began its move westward in 1855 as the southwest branch of the Pacific Railroad stretched as far as Rolla by 1860. The Civil War brought further westward construction to a halt. Loaded with debt, several re-incorporations resulted in the St. Louis-San Francisco Railway Company, more commonly known as the Frisco, in 1868. One of its two main lines, the St. Louis-to-Tulsa route, cut right through the Gascosage area.

In a scenario that would play out time and again as the railroad spread across the West, towns sprang up along the way, in some cases replacing the villages that preceded them. One such village sprang up when the men hired to cut and haul cordwood to fuel the railroad's engines began building log cabins for homes. To claim the village as their own, they actually formed a company called Nelson and Company, purchasing and platting forty acres for the village they named Woodend. In the coming decades, a great many Swedes migrated to the village and having become the majority nationality by 1883, they renamed the growing village Swedeborg.

In another case, a trading post named Humboldt gave way to the town of Crocker when the railroad built a freight depot in 1869 about a mile southeast of the trading post. The depot in Crocker served as a mail pick-up and distribution point for twenty-two surrounding towns. By 1871 the businesses surrounding the trading post relocated to Crocker and Humboldt was abandoned.

The people of Crocker send off their soldiers at the depot during WWI. *Photo courtesy of Pulaski County Historical Society.*

A roundhouse, constructed to provide the trains with a helper engine in order to climb the higher elevations of the plateau, resulted in the town of Newburg. The switch, built between Newburg and

Main Street, looking south, in Crocker, Missouri. *Photo courtesy of Pulaski County Historical Society.*

The old Frisco Railroad Station as it sat along the railroad line in Crocker. *Photo courtesy of Pulaski County Historical Society.*

Crocker High School outing, 1900. *Photo courtesy of Pulaski County Historical Society.*

A horse and buggy crosses the first bridge across the Gasconade River connecting Crocker and Waynesville. *Photo courtesy of Pulaski County Historical Society.*

Dixon for the helper engines, was quickly accompanied by a depot, a telegraph office, and a few stores, creating the village known as Frank's Switch.

In 1869, surveyor Milton Santee laid out the towns of Richland and Dixon. Although a number of nearby settlements older than Dixon survived the Civil War period, the first large settlement near the town itself was a camp just to the west consisting of about one hundred workers who were working on the railroad in 1867–1868. Later, the workers moved into town. As Mr. Santee platted it, the original town of Dixon straddled the railroad tracks, a half-mile on each side, and consisted of three stores, one gristmill, three hotels, one church, a public school, and a few homes. Around 1873, Dixon became a railroad division point with eating and housing facilities for four freight crews and three passenger crews. Three years later the division point was moved to St. James, then returned to Dixon in 1878. In 1884 the division point was permanently moved to Newburg and though it was a blow to Dixon's

Dixon farmers during WWI. *Photo courtesy of Pulaski County Historical Society.*

economy, citizens in surrounding communities continued to bring wheat, hogs, cattle, sheep, furs, wild game, and produce to Dixon to be shipped on the Frisco.

Mr. Santee laid out the city of Richland in the same manner as Dixon, straddling the railroad tracks that brought it to life. In early 1870 the Richland Institute was established, a private academy built by a private stock company in which almost every member of the community had a financial interest. Both the institute and the city were named after G. W. Rich, director of the Frisco Railroad. The institute survived until the early 1900s when it was absorbed into the public school system.

Which came first, the railroad or the people? That's nearly impossible to say, but the jobs the railroad created continued to spur growth beyond the initial settlers. Among the railroad workers were people of varied nationalities and one gentleman who recalled those early days of the railroad boasted that he "gained three sons-in-law from the coming of the railroad: an Irishman, an Englishman, and a German."

Historic Route 66 has had several names throughout its life. Once trod by migrating mastodon and Native Americans in search of game, it was first known as the Osage Indian Trail. By the mid-1800s, it became known as the Wire Road for the telegraph lines that followed it. The messages transmitted along the lines were as important during the Civil War as the troops and materials that traversed the road itself. When finally paved in the 1920s, it became a major access road for tourists heading to Lake Ozark and spawned numerous tourist-related businesses along the way.

The coming of the railroad and the roads created a means for the farmers to receive the goods they needed and made it possible for them to get their own wares to market, making subsistence farming a thing of the past for the people of Gascosage.

Still, life on the farm wasn't for the feint of heart, and it would be a long time before it would get any easier.

The train arrives at Dixon. *Photo courtesy of Pulaski County Historical Society.*

## The So-Called Good Old Days

From a twenty-first century perspective, it's easy to romanticize life in rural America. But without the laborsaving devices that electricity now provides, everything was done with backbreaking labor. Gascosage member Ethel M. Plunkett wrote about the difficulties of carving out a life in the rugged Ozark hills before the days of electricity:

Work on the farm meant backbreaking labor. Eventually electricity made many tasks much easier. *Photo courtesy of* Rural Missouri.

> *Life in earlier days amid the Ozarks was meager and often grim. Food was limited to what could be produced on the land. Each farm home had its small flock of chickens and the eggs were treated as nuggets of gold. The returns from them were used to purchase sugar, coffee and a bit of "chawin tobaccer." Fortunately the woods and fields yielded wild berries of different varieties and in abundant quantities. These were gathered by the women and children and were canned or made into jellies and jams.*
>
> *Food was only cooked in warm weather as required to prevent spoilage. One visiting minister was said to remark that some of the best fried chicken he had ever eaten had met him on foot a short time previously. Houseflies were combated with little success because many homes could not afford screens. In summertime when the table was laid for a meal, plates were always inverted so this household pest would not contaminate them. These courageous people did their best for the health of their families that conditions would allow.*

Daylight was precious and to save time farmers often took their midday meal out in the field.

Local resident R. B. Thompson was interviewed in 1969 when Dixon celebrated its centennial. Like his hometown, he was one hundred years old at the time. He recalled watching his father plow with oxen and eating the cornpone his mother made in the fireplace by setting her skillet on a bed of coals and piling more coals on the lid. Lessons were read by "grease light," a wick placed in a dish of animal fat. The school year only lasted three or four months a year when work on the farm allowed it. As a younger man, he and his brother provided the merry-go-round for Dixon's picnics in the park. The ride was steam driven and had its own music coming from an organ played mechanically by a leather belt hooked to the engine. "It took five wagons to haul the ride," he said, "and another team just for the engine which was on wheels." He reported making $200 with it in one day at a time when people were glad to work for 50¢ a day.

When interviewed for a 1968 article in the *Rural Electric Missourian*, long-time Dixon resident W. A. Grempczynski, age eighty, recalled the days before electricity: "I remember three kinds of lights in our store," he said, referring to the large dry goods store his family operated for fifty-six years. His father died when he was in eighth grade and he started working full time. "The lights we had then were coal oil. They made a reddish light and they smoked so much they had to be cleaned every other day. When we got gaslights we thought that was a great improvement because they gave a much brighter, clearer light and all we had to do for them was pump them up with air every day, fifteen minutes or so of work. Of course, when we got electricity, then we knew what seeing and convenience really was."

To do laundry, women had to haul water from the creek and heat it over a wood fire. *Photo courtesy of* Rural Missouri.

In a book titled *The Day the Lights Came On* published by the Missouri Rural Electric Women's Association in 2000, Newburg resident Mary Agnes Hudson described the arduous task of washing and ironing clothes during the days before electricity: "There was no push button washing machine. You were the washing machine. A rub board, bar of lye soap and strong hands and back

Before electricity, flat irons (otherwise known as sad irons) had to be heated on wood stoves. *Photo courtesy of* Rural Missouri.

were the only requirements to hook up to that energy source. The dryer was a line in the yard you pinned clothes to. The sun and air took care of the rest. Then you built a fire in the kitchen (wood burning) stove. You set flat irons on the stove to heat. Then you touched the bottom of the iron with a moistened finger. If it sizzled it was ready for the heavy garments."

When asked if she'd like to go back to the "good old days," she replied, "Not without being forced to. Any good memory makes good old days."

When Dixon was first founded, most settlers used homemade tallow candles for lighting. One lady known as "Aunt Polly" Miller often told the story of how she and her husband lighted their first kerosene lamp standing far away from it using a homemade broom.

The first electric light plant in Dixon dated to about 1909. Its location by the "old Dixon Pond" made it a convenient place for the wintertime skaters to go in to warm up. Mr. Grempczynski remembered Dixon's first electric lights were only turned on for a few hours and went off at 11 o'clock every night. "They blinked them three times at a quarter 'till," he said, "so you'd be prepared for them to go off. If you were at a party, you knew exactly when to start putting your coat on."

Retired right-of-way foreman Bill Thompson recalled growing up in Alder Springs near Iberia. "We'd get up and carry an old lantern out to milk the cows and by that time Mom would have breakfast done. She'd have a lamp setting in the middle of the table. I guess we ate good food—we couldn't see it. By daylight, we were ready to go."

During the Great Depression, people had little money to buy the produce and meat the farmers produced and one of the worst droughts in the country's history just added to their troubles. Though just a young child, current board member Bill Davis recalls his own grandfather working for the Works Progress Administration making eighteen cents an hour. "During the Depression, people couldn't have afforded to have a house wired," he said. His Sunday job was to prepare for washday on Monday so he'd "draw water from the well, fill the wash kettle with water and bust up some firewood." The next morning before leaving for school, he'd start the fire to heat the water.

The editorial in the December 21, 1935, edition of the *St. Louis Star Times* read, "It is a staggering commentary on the backwardness of rural life in the State that there were still 238,047 farms in Missouri at the beginning of 1935 not supplied with electric current. More than a quarter of a million Missouri farms where electric light is unknown; where churning butter is household drudgery and milking cows by hand a chore; where hair curlers must be heated over a smoky kerosene lamp chimney when ma and the girls go to town." The president of the Consumers' Cooperative Association of North Kansas City proclaimed in January of 1936: "A higher proportion of pig-pens in Sweden are lighted by electricity than the ratio of farm homes with electricity in the United States." ■

---


**Sources:**

*The Day the Lights Came On*, Missouri Rural Electric Women's Association, 2000, Jim McCarty, editor.

Dixon Centennial Souvenir Book, published in 1969 by the Dixon Advancement Association, Luther Riddle, president.

http://www.visitpulaskicounty.org/Brochures/rt662006.pdf

Hanging the transform on the F. R. Holtsclaw place south of Dixon off Highway D, residen engineer B. E. Shaw observes Forbes George and Charles Sooter at the top of the pole.

CHAPTER TWO

# A New Deal, A New Era

■ During the Great Depression, people in American cities lined up at soup kitchens and farmers across America battled the worst drought in history. Many young rural men took jobs with the Civilian Conservation Corps and the Works Progress Administration, sending home the majority of their meager earnings to save the family farm from foreclosure. Philosophical differences broiled in Congress as legislators wrestled with the issue of how much help Uncle Sam should be expected to extend and to what degree people should be expected to "pull themselves up by their own bootstraps." The reformers among Congress won out and in 1935 a second round of New Deal legislation was enacted. However, this time the legislation was geared less on relief and more on creating avenues for sustainable change. The Resettlement Administration was formed as a land resource management agency moving farmers from subsistence land to more fertile ground. In some areas, suburban developments sprang up for the resettlement of farmers displaced by the Great Depression. By 1937 the Resettlement Administration was reorganized under the Agriculture Department as the Farm Security Administration and redirected its resources toward offering loans, grants, and agricultural education.

While Missouri farmers weren't directly impacted by passage of the Tennessee Valley Act in 1933, it certainly helped to shed light on the problems they faced. TVA authorized the construction of a dam, later named Norris Dam for the Nebraska senator who lobbied for it, intended to provide farmers relief from depleted soil and periodic flooding. But the most dramatic change for farmers would come from the electricity generated by TVA dams, increasing the awareness of the benefits of electricity not just for rural Americans' personal standard of living, but the production capabilities of their farms as well.

## The Rural Electrification Administration

EXECUTIVE ORDER

ESTABLISHMENT OF THE RURAL ELECTRIFICATION ADMINISTRATION

*By virtue of and pursuant to the authority vested in me under the Emergency Relief Appropriation Act of 1935, approved April 8, 1935 (Public Resolution No. 11, 74th Congress), I hereby establish an agency within the Government to be known as the "Rural Electrification Administration", the head thereof to be known as the Administrator.*

*I hereby prescribe the following duties and functions of the said Rural Electrification Administration to be exercised and performed by the Administrator thereof to be hereafter appointed:*

*To initiate, formulate, administer, and supervise a program of approved projects with respect to the generation, transmission, and distribution of electric energy in rural areas.*

*In the performance of such duties and functions, expenditures are hereby authorized for necessary supplies and equipment; law books and books of reference, directories, periodicals, newspapers and press clippings; travel expenses, including the expense of attendance at meetings when specifically authorized by the Administrator; rental at the seat of Government and elsewhere; purchase, operation and maintenance of passenger-carrying vehicles; printing and binding; and incidental expenses; and I hereby authorize the Administrator to accept and utilize such voluntary and uncompensated services and, with the consent of the State, such State and local officers and employees, and appoint, without regard to the provisions of the civil service laws, such officers and employees, as may be necessary, prescribe their duties and responsibilities and, without regard to the Classification Act of 1923, as amended, fix their compensation:* **Provided,** *That in so far as practicable, the persons employed under the authority of this Executive Order shall be selected from those receiving relief.*

*To the extent necessary to carry out the provisions of this Executive Order the Administrator is authorized to acquire, by purchase or by the power of eminent domain, any real property or any interest therein and improve, develop, grant, sell, lease (with or without the privilege of purchasing), or otherwise dispose of any such property or interest therein*

*For the administrative expenses of the Rural Electrification Administration there is hereby allocated to the Administration from the appropriation made by the Emergency Relief Appropriation Act of 1935 the sum of $75,000. Allocations will be made hereafter for authorized projects.*

*The White House,*
*May 11, 1935*

*7037*

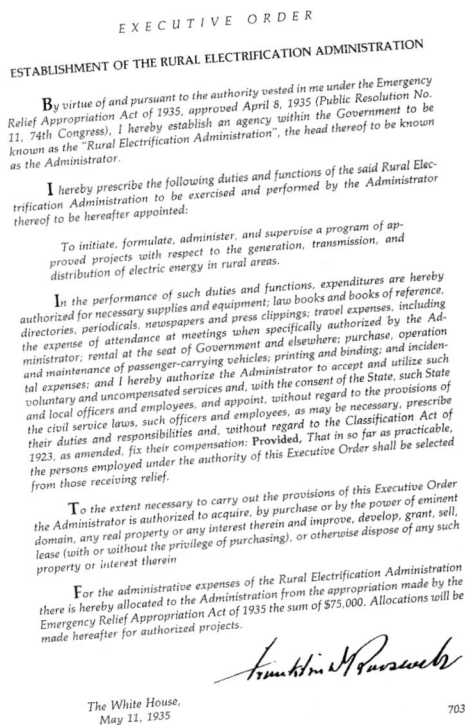

Executive order No. 7037, creating the REA, reflected President Roosevelt's belief that people were better off with a "hand up" instead of a "hand out." *Photo courtesy of* Rural Missouri.

President Franklin Delano Roosevelt issued executive order No. 7037 creating the Rural Electrification Administration on May 11, 1935, under authority of the Emergency Relief Appropriation Act of 1935. As part of the reforms initiated through the second wave of New Deal legislation, the Rural Electrification Administration was part of a relief package designed to stimulate the rural economies by bringing them into the modern era. They believed that providing rural farmers with electricity would not only improve their lives but also provide them with the means to increase their productivity. Roosevelt's belief, reflected in the legislation, was that individuals fared better when provided with an opportunity for self-reliance.

Representative John E. Rankin of Mississippi and Senator George William Norris of Nebraska were united in their concern for the lives of rural Americans, despite their philosophical and political differences, and proposed the idea for the REA. Senator Norris later became known as the Father of the Tennessee Valley Authority. The following year, Congress passed the Norris-Rayburn

Act appropriating $410 million for a ten-year program.

Only two restrictions were placed on the cooperatives: they would not be allowed to compete directly with investor-owned utility companies and no one living in a city with a population of 1,500 or more could be a co-op member. In 1939 the REA was reorganized as a division of the U.S. Department of Agriculture.

## A Screeching Halt

Just as the REA was gaining momentum across the country, the United States entered World War II. The War Production Board decided copper wire was more critical for the war effort than for rural power lines and pulled the proverbial plug on rural electrification. In a stunning contradiction, the government was asking farmers to increase their productivity to feed the hungry troops, at the same time they were denying them the one thing intended to help them do just that—electricity.

The government's drive to accumulate enough metal for the war effort halted the purchase of wires, poles, transformers, and meters. Any project that was 40 percent or more complete by December 5, 1941, could be finished. All other projects were brought to a halt. However, realizing they needed farms to be productive in order to feed the troops and the American population, the War Production Board struck a compromise they called the farm unit plan. Under that plan, farms were energized based on their livestock holdings, a plan that continued until after the war. Occasionally, one farmer's holdings were substantial enough to allow them to build enough line to get to the next farm. The rumors were that livestock was sometimes strategically moved on the days the inspectors arrived in order to keep the lines coming.

## Getting Organized

As long as World War II was occupying the nation's attention and its efforts, farmers in the area reconciled themselves to life without electricity. However, once the war was over and VJ Day celebrations came to a close, discussions once again picked up regarding the possibility. At the time, the city of Dixon was already receiving electricity from Sho-Me Power Corporation. Mr. Skaggs, who owned the power plant by the old Dixon Pond, had sold it to Sho-Me back in 1925.

At the time the closest REA cooperatives were located at Licking, Lebanon, and Linn, Missouri. While they surrounded the Gascosage area, these co-ops had their hands full stretching scarce materials to serve the farmers in their own territories.

A few men who'd assumed leadership among the farmers wrote to the REA, which was headquartered in St. Louis at the time. The REA did a study deeming the project feasible and sent a field man to furnish information on how to get organized.

According to one account, it was on September 5, 1945, that the REA man stopped at a filling station south of Dixon. "This is nice country, but you don't have electricity," he remarked to the attendant. "Oh, no. We'll never get anything like that in these hills," replied the man. "You might get a surprise!" the REA man retorted.

These men drove throughout the countryside, visiting friends and neighbors, trying to convince them to pay their five dollars and sign up as a member of the cooperative. The reception they got was mixed. Some folks were eager to get on board and some were fearful of something they didn't understand. Some didn't have the five dollars regardless of how they felt about getting electricity. Former lineman Jim Williams recalled being told of one man who said, "I'll give the $5.00 but I don't think it'll ever amount to anything."

Nonetheless, those farm leaders prevailed and became the incorporators and first board of directors of Missouri 68 Gascosage Electric Cooperative. Only one more rural electric cooperative would be organized in the state of Missouri. They held their first meeting in Dixon's city hall on September 24, 1945. Joseph B. Lischwe presided as president and Victor D. Street acted as secretary. The other seven directors and original incorporators included Willard Humphrey, L. W. Keeth, John

## The Next Greatest Thing

■ To understand just how truly significant the trademarked "REA Co-op" sign was to America's farmers, there is a story told by a man who worked for the Tennessee Valley Authority as a land buyer. Traveling a country road one evening in the early 1940s he came upon a farmer sitting on a little knoll overlooking his farmhouse, which had recently been electrified. The land buyer noticed the look of wonder on the man's face as he gazed at the lighted windows of his home and the light shining on the path to the barn. A few days later, the TVA man attended the church to which this farmer belonged. When the preacher asked the congregation to give witness, the farmer stood and said, "Brothers and sisters, I want to tell you this. The greatest thing on earth is to have the love of God in your heart, and the next greatest thing is to have electricity in your house."

**Source:**

Mitchell, Bob. Newspaper column entitled "Ozark Views and Comments," *Cassville Democrat*, October 14, 2009.

Woolery, Ferrell H. Roam, Barney Stokes, A. W. Davis, and Adam E. Copeland. The bylaws and corporate seal were adopted, forms were selected for application for membership, action was taken regarding insurance and signing of checks, and an engineer was selected. Midwestern Engineers of Tulsa, Oklahoma, was chosen to prepare pre-allotment maps and provide engineering services for the cooperative. Annual meetings were set for the fourth Thursday in September of each year, beginning in 1946.

1948 Gascosage Board of Directors. Left to right: Adam E. Copeland, John Woolery, Ferrell H. Roam, Don Bartelt, Joseph B. Lischwe, Willard Humphrey, Victor D. Street, Barney Stokes, and Manager Luther A. Riddle.

The following month, Homer Hill of the Applications and Loans Division of the REA met with the board to give them instructions on mapping and the submission of loan requests. The funds were available, he told them, and getting their application and documentation in on time would expedite the receipt of their first loan for $206,995.

1949 Gascosage Board of Directors. Seated: Manager Luther Riddle and Joseph Lischwe. Standing: Ferrell H. Roam, Sherman Denton, Don Bartelt, Barney Stokes, Victor Street, and Adam Copeland. Clyde Bilyeu is not pictured.

Setting poles and stringing electrical lines were new for the men of Gascosage as it was for most men in the rural areas across the country. To help out, the REA drafted plans and set engineering standards. To make the funding reach as far as possible, the REA saw to it that the specifications were as economical as possible. Materials were standardized to provide economies of scale for the materials suppliers.

REA crews traveled through the American countryside installing wiring in houses and barns. A standard REA installation in a house consisted of a 60-amp, 230-volt fuse panel with a 60-amp range circuit, a 20-amp kitchen circuit, and two or three 15-amp lighting circuits. A ceiling-mounted light fixture was installed in each room, controlled either by a pull chain or a single switch mounted near a door. Electrical appliances were scarce so, at most, one outlet was installed in each room.

Trees were cut with a crosscut saw to clear the right-of-way, holes were dug with a banjo and a spoon, and poles were set by hand using an A-frame. Now and then, the process required a bit of rest. *Photo courtesy of Juanita Barnett of Iberia.*

Workers from a St. Louis engineering firm (possibly WPA workers) use a banjo and a spoon to dig holes near Iberia. *Photo courtesy of Juanita Barnett of Iberia.*

Stringing wire on Bill Shackleford property south of Dixon, 1948. Left to right: Charles Sooter on the pole, Orville Griffin, Theodore Woolery, Ramond Mitchell, and Harvey Humphrey.

Like any newcomer, Gascosage had to find its place among existing power providers. In November of 1945 the board learned that Sho-Me Power Corporation was willing to sell its interests, including 450 consumers, in Miller, Pulaski, and Maries Counties to Gascosage for $140,512. In addition, Sho-Me was willing to lease some of its electric distribution facilities to provide a more effective coordination between Sho-Me and Gascosage. Laclede Electric Cooperative of Lebanon owned and operated lines that were nearer Dixon than Lebanon and would therefore be better served by Gascosage. Negotiations began and on April 29, 1946, Gascosage purchased Laclede's distribution system in Iberia; the 6.9 kV distribution line from Crocker to Iberia; and the 6.9 kV distribution line from Crocker south 3.3 miles, serving 148 members with an annual revenue just under $10,000. Laclede's asking price was $15,000 plus the cost of recently made capital additions totaling $2,726.

In the meantime, the board received word from the REA in March of 1946 that they would receive an allotment for 150 miles of line instead of the 200 they included on their mapping plan. They selected an engineering firm, H. B. Gieb and Associates of Dallas, Texas, to build the first section of 150 miles of line. On June 18, 1946, they received their first loan contract for $206,995 to finance construction of transmission and distribution lines, approved the following November.

It was time to actually set up an office and officially open for business. At the April 1, 1946, board meeting, five applicants for the manager's position were each given five minutes to present themselves. Luther Riddle was selected as their first choice among the five candidates.

Luther Riddle was born and raised on Jones Creek near the Riddle Bridge named for his grandfather, Eliza Riddle. For a while, he taught

Seventy-five members attended the second annual meeting at the Dixon Theatre in 1948.

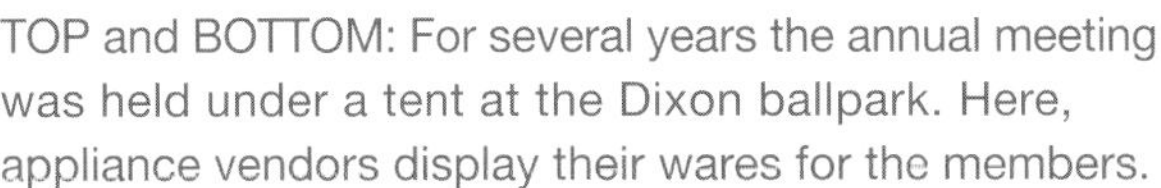

TOP and BOTTOM: For several years the annual meeting was held under a tent at the Dixon ballpark. Here, appliance vendors display their wares for the members.

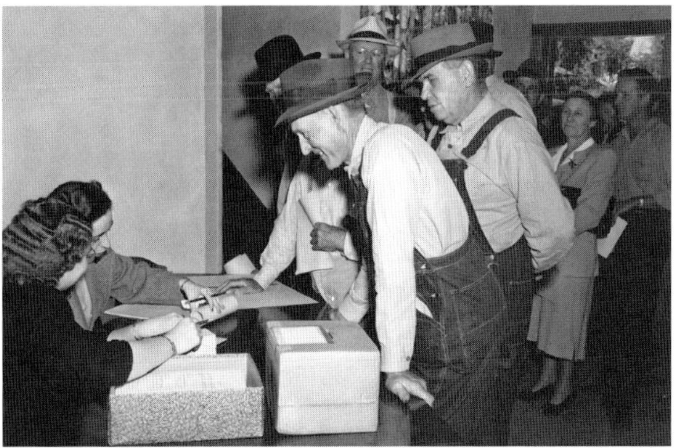

TOP: Inside the theatre at Gascosage's second annual meeting in Dixon on September 28, 1948.

BOTTOM: Delores Humphrey Eads and Mary June Hamilton register members at the 1948 annual meeting.

## Mule Power

■ One of the toughest parts of building those early lines was pulling the heavy lines the mile or so between poles over terrain that was often rocky and hilly. Gene Allen recalled the time they were building a line east of Crocker on terrain that was so steep the men could barely walk it. When a nearby farmer offered the use of his mules, despite the farmer's warning about the mules' untamed nature, they couldn't resist the four-legged laborsaving device. "We got the mule set," Gene said, "and my cousin Lloyd Allen was foreman so he decided that he would ride it. Well, there's no telling how high that mule threw him." Eventually they got the harness on the mule and hooked the wire to it. Gene's dad Henry was leading the mule and Lloyd and Gene were walking alongside the wire to keep it straight. Henry insisted on walking on the lower side of the mule and because of the steep terrain, the mule kept crowding down on him. Lloyd said, "Henry, why don't you get on the upper side of that mule so it won't be getting on you all the time?" Gene said his dad thought about how the mule had thrown Lloyd earlier and replied, "Lloyd, I'd rather that mule be on me than me be on it."

at area schools making about $40 a month and then attended college at the School of Mines in Rolla and Washington University in St. Louis majoring in business and public administration. While in St. Louis, he joined the naval reserves and in 1940 was called to active duty in the U.S. Navy. He worked in aviation, radio, a new-fangled invention called radar, and as an electrician during his five years of service. In 1945 Luther returned home from the navy and was headed to Kansas City to find work at the Federal Aviation Administration when A. W. Davis, one of the original directors of the co-op, suggested he apply for the manager's job at Gascosage.

The board's choice for manager received REA approval and Luther was instructed to assume his duties as manager on June 17, 1946, at a salary of $200 per month. He was also to purchase necessary office furniture, fixtures, supplies, and equipment; to rent an office; and purchase a truck. He selected an office in a building owned by Edwin "Birdie" Russell in Dixon, purchased a 1½-ton truck, and with his customary frugality, scrounged the rest. "There weren't any desks available so I went down to the bank and Ray Stevens gave me a desk," Luther recalled years later. "Then I went down to Gilbert's Furniture Store and bought two chairs. I gave $2.00 a piece for them." Myrtle Creech was hired as the first office employee and Robert E. Smith as lineman. The board agreed to pay Luther 5¢ per mile to use his own automobile and agreed to compensate themselves $3.00 for each meeting attended and 5¢ per mile for traveling to and from meetings.

They were starting a new business from the ground up and a lot of decisions had to be made, particularly where customer service was involved. The board decided the cooperative would furnish the meter, meter socket, and all wiring on the service pole including a service breaker if a service pole was installed. If a meter was to be placed on the house, the cooperative would furnish the meter and meter socket only. They also decided to have a cooperative employee do the house wiring inspection at the time of meter installation at no cost to the member. In addition, the co-op's southwest boundaries were extended along the south border of Township 37 to the southwest corner of Section 35, Range 9, then north on section line to northern boundary of Township 39, then west to Gasconade River. On March 19, 1947, they extended the boundary further to include Phelps County.

The first lines delivering power purchased from Sho-Me Power Corporation were built in 1947 to provide twenty-five miles of electric service to consumers near Iberia. By that fall, about twenty-five people on approximately twenty miles of line near Iberia received electricity for the first time and were Gascosage's first consumers. The first family to "turn on the lights" lived on Highway 17 and Luther Riddle recalled their stunned reaction. "I told them they could turn on the electric," he said, "but the family was eating dinner at the time and they were afraid to turn on the power. So I flipped the switch and a light came on over the table. The wife's first reaction was 'It's too bright, turn it down.'"

Two eras meet as a horse and buggy halts at a substation near Iberia. *Photo courtesy of Juanita Barnett of Iberia.*

Though the board originally intended to begin annual meetings in 1946, the first was held on September 25, 1947, in the co-op's office. Manager Riddle proudly reported, "Today we are operating nearly thirteen miles of line and are serving 270 customers in Miller and Pulaski Counties. Your Cooperative has under construction twenty-eight miles of rural line to serve seventy-seven customers and final plans for the construction of a total of 200 miles of rural line. In addition, your Cooperative has received approval for the construction of 200 more miles making a total of 400 miles to serve rural farms."

One of the co-op's first offices was in this building in downtown Dixon next door to Veasman Hardware.

The co-op moved to a new location in 1947, in a building east of Veasman Hardware. (In 1953, the co-op's office moved a couple doors down to Dixon's American Legion Building.) Three office positions were added: Mary June Hamilton was bookkeeper, Deloris Humphrey Eads was billing clerk, and Norma Veasman was hired as secretary. In August of that year, Luther explained in a newspaper article, "Material orders have been placed approximately one year ago for the construction of 200 miles of line." Slow delivery of materials was causing consternation among those folks who were now more eager than ever to enjoy the benefits of electricity. Invoking the REA's "area coverage program" based on the belief that every farmer and rural homeowner was entitled to highline electric service, Luther assured them they would receive electricity as soon as humanly possible. ■

Clint Bays and Forbes George in front of the Gascosage office displaying a hawk the removed from a line, still clutching its quarr

CHAPTER THREE

# A Period of Growth

■ In the years between 1947 and 1956, Gascosage Electric Cooperative more than doubled its miles of line and expanded well into Maries County. Manager Luther Riddle was instrumental in the expansion of rural electric service and at his urging the board of directors joined the state and national associations to participate in regional and national issues. Barney Stokes and A. W. Davis were selected to be the first to represent Gascosage at the state association meeting on January 3, 1947.

By 1947, material shortages were no longer a problem; ironically, the very success of the rural electrification program was causing its own obstacles. A July 11, 1947, headline read, "Power Shortage Biggest Factor Retarding REA." William J. Neal, deputy administrator of the REA in Washington, D.C., predicted the construction programs of the majority of REA cooperatives were likely to be stalled soon because of the lack of power.

As of May 1948 the co-op identified approximately 198 prospective members who were without electric service even though they were within five thousand feet of existing lines. The board applied to the REA for a loan for $135,000 to be used to build approximately seventy-five miles of three-phase electric distribution lines to these new members.

Attending the second annual meeting held in the old Dixon Theater building on September 25, 1948, were 75 members with 175 family members and friends. The featured guest, Dr. Forrest Brown of Iberia Junior College, praised the farmers for the advancements they'd seen in recent years as a result of the electrification of the farms, which came about largely through their cooperative efforts. To keep their expanding membership informed and continue their education on the uses of electricity, the board opted to subscribe to *Rural Electric Missourian* on behalf of its consumers, paying fifty-five cents per year out of the co-op's general funds for each consumer who wished to subscribe.

Attendance prizes at the 1948 meeting included electric lamps, waffle irons, toasters, and lamps.

With deliveries of materials improving, plans were made in September of 1948 for staking an additional 150 miles of rural lines in Maries, Miller, Phelps, and Pulaski Counties. In the Dixon area alone, about forty miles of new lines were under construction. The lines ran north along Highway 28 to the Hayden Road with branch lines extending into the Clifty Dale community, Maries Valley Road, and extending westward along Highway 133 to the Fox Crossing community, running south along Highway 28 to Portuguese Point with branch lines extending into the Pisgah, Franks, and Santee communities. The estimated cost of construction of this forty miles, including a new substation installed south of Dixon, was approximately $65,000. To complete all this work, Gascosage was able to obtain a new loan for $465,005. "As a result of this loan," the board announced, "the Cooperative will be able to build new lines to 500 rural farms, schools, churches, and rural industries, and also improve the service of the consumers the Cooperative is now serving. Upon completion of its present building plans, the system will be increased to 600 miles of rural lines serving 1800 consumers."

## Willie Wiredhand

■ A man named Ashton Collins created Reddy Kilowatt with his familiar lightning bolt body in 1926. When the REA considered adopting Reddy as their own mascot, Collins, who regarded the co-ops as socialistic, denied them permission to use Reddy, reserving him for "investor-owned, tax-paying" utilities.

Andrew McLay, an entomologist turned artist who later worked for the National Rural Electric Cooperative Association (NRECA), created Willie Wiredhand to be the mascot for rural co-ops across the country on October 30, 1950. Several years later, a group of privately owned utilities, along with Ashton Collins, filed a federal lawsuit against Willie. In January 1956, a U.S. District Court denied Reddy his monopoly after a weeklong trial. The phrase, "He's small, but he's wirey," came out of that trial between Willie Wiredhand and Reddy Kilowatt, a conflict that became a symbol for the tension that existed between the co-ops and the commercial power companies.

Willie Wiredhand became part of virtually every publication, advertisement, and display associated with rural electric cooperatives.

Continuing in the spirit of expansion, the co-op opted to rent the extension of the building adjoining their office building for warehouse space in October of 1948. Plans were also underway to rewire the city of Iberia. However, despite the fact that funds had been appropriated for the project, the board announced they could not justify investing the $40,000 to $50,000 it would cost without a franchise commitment. In October of 1948, the citizens of Iberia gave Gascosage their vote of confidence and granted the twenty-year franchise.

The rural electrification program was showing signs of continued success. In 1935 when the Rural Electrification Act was first signed, one out of ten American farms was electrified. By 1948, six out of ten American farms were enjoying the benefits of electricity. The success and growth of rural electrification was not without challenges, and the shortage of power first mentioned publicly in 1947 was now being addressed.

Sho-Me Power Corporation offered many lectures on electricity. This one was at the Dixon High School in the 1950s.

In May of 1949, directors and representatives from over two hundred cooperatives throughout Missouri, Arkansas, Kansas, Oklahoma, Texas, and Louisiana went to Washington, D.C., to unite their efforts toward providing the southwest region with adequate, dependable, and low-cost

Employees Loran Humphrey, Lloyd Allen, Walter Whitaker, and Skip Martin use an A-frame to set a pole.

electric power. The consensus among them was that the most efficient and cost-effective way to accomplish this was through the Southwestern Power Administration (SPA). Many of the rural cooperatives, Gascosage among them, went to work lobbying for their support. The minutes of the April 20, 1949, board meeting authorized Luther Riddle to attend these meetings in Washington, D.C., and to "support with all effort the program of Southwestern Power Administration, in securing funds for the building of transmission lines into South and Southwest Missouri to furnish power to public utilities and power stranded cooperatives. Also that the building of the transmission lines would not duplicate any lines that are now built and would help lines which are now at capacity." The Bureau of the Federal Budget approved Southwestern Power Administration's request for a loan necessary to transmit the electric power from the government dams to the rural cooperatives.

The function of the REA was expanded in 1949 when it received authorization to loan funds for developing telephone service in rural areas. Gascosage's board of directors gave Luther the authority to execute joint use agreements with local telephone companies for the use of their poles. At the 1950 annual meeting W. A. Murphy of the Triangle Telephone Company, which served Dixon, Crocker, and Iberia, announced this new function of the REA and asked members to return the applications for telephone service they'd recently mailed to residents in the area. A map showing the location of those who were requesting telephone service was to be prepared and sent to the REA along with their request for a loan to extend the telephone system into the rural areas. Even as late as 1959, many rural folks in the Gascosage area were waiting for telephone service and the co-op continued to help wherever possible.

Downtown Dixon, Missouri, in the early 1950s.

## Annual Meetings

In 1949 and 1950, Gascosage's annual meetings were held in the present Dixon Middle School Gymnasium with attendance prizes given away. For the next few years after that, the meetings were held under tents at the Dixon ballpark. The tents, and often the entertainment that traveled with them, were provided by the REA. Folks came to enjoy the visit with neighbors and friends, taking time to peruse the appliance displays set up by local dealers.

An estimated six hundred people attended the 1950 annual meeting. The co-op's progress report from the previous three years got a round of applause from the crowd when Manager Luther Riddle presented his report. "In three years of operation, the co-op has boosted membership from 365 to 1,602," he said. Five hundred and fifteen miles of line were constructed and the annual purchase of wholesale kilowatts by the co-op increased from 360,000 in 1948 to 1,127,854 in 1950. "For the improvement of service to farms already connected the Cooperative has installed a number of automatic circuit breakers, which limits outages to small sections of line under ordinary circumstances. These new breakers, along with our increased substation capacity, should mean better service to every member of the cooperative."

Manager Luther Riddle presents graphs showing the co-op's growth, 1955.

Victor Street, secretary/treasurer of the co-op, announced the value of the distribution plant was $678,472.25, placing the total assets of the organization at $974,242.89. Featured speaker, F. V. Heinkel, president of the Missouri Farmer's Association, advised members to "keep those bright boys on the farm and maintain a farm family" by electrifying. "Farm boys and girls are no longer, after having attended modern high schools and colleges, going

Inside the co-op's first office, employees Mary June Hamilton (back) and Norma Veasman Riddle go to work, 1950.

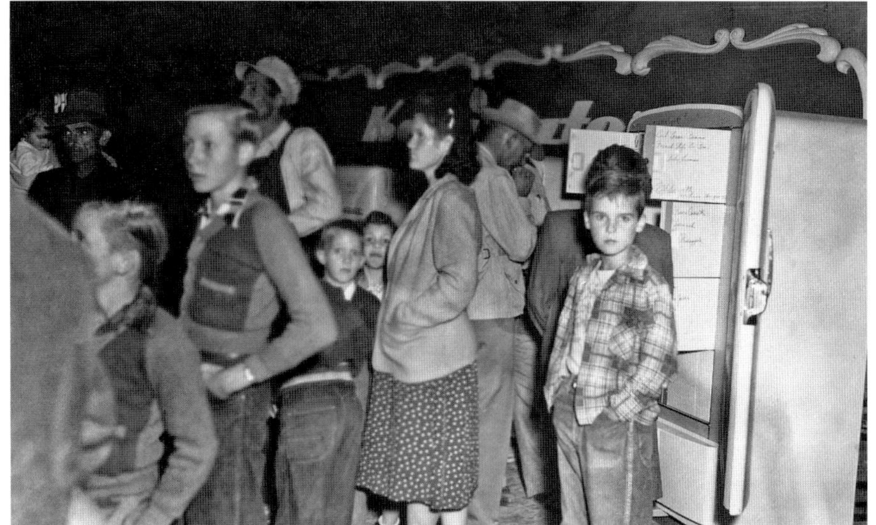

Gascosage's annual meetings have always been family events.

The board of directors always had the stage for the annual meetings, but the attendance prizes were front and center.

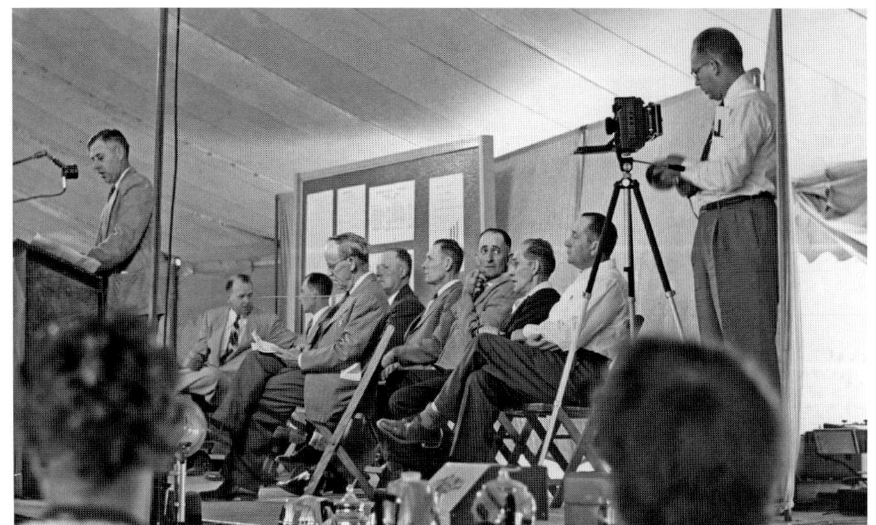

A *St. Louis Post Dispatch* photographer took this picture at the September 24, 1954, annual meeting. Seated behind Luther Riddle at the podium are attorney Gregory Stockard and board members Don Bartelt, Ferrel Roam, Sherman Denton, Leonard Keeth, Fred McDonald, Euell Penland, and Joe Lischwe.

Luther Riddle opens the 1955 annual meeting under the tent.

Directors Adam Copeland, Sherman Denton, and Don Bartelt at the annual meeting.

back to live on the farm under primitive conditions," he cautioned. Mr. Heinkel repeatedly warned REA members to fight and work for their organization. "We (the farmers) did not have electricity before the REA," he said, charging that private companies who once refused to build lines to farmers were now protesting the cooperatives.

In October of 1950, Gascosage "turned on the lights" for three new areas—the Franks community, near the Pisgah community, and in the Brinktown district. The work was done by the Drew Construction Company with an estimated force of sixty men on the job. While these areas were just then being energized, Luther Riddle commented on the changing attitudes toward electricity at the 1951 annual meeting. "We've gone from 0 to 90% in just four years," he said. "Five years ago we couldn't even get the farmers to talk with us about it. It was just an added expense. Today the average farmer takes for granted the use of electric lights, refrigerators, irons, and washing machines and is beginning to make use of electricity increasingly for pump systems, milkers, brooders and other equipment." By 1951, Gascosage members were using an average of 133 kWh per month, up from an average of only 50 kWh in 1949. Also in 1951 Gascosage installed a two-way Motorola radio system with five mobile units available for emergency services.

Shortly after the 1951 annual meeting, the Missouri Public Service Commission gave Gascosage approval to finally purchase the Sho-Me electrical distribution systems in the area. The

## 1951 Annual Meeting Program

■ The program for the 1951 annual meeting included some useful tidbits of information regarding the efficiency that electricity afforded the average farmer:

Did you know that one kilowatt-hour of electricity will...

Pump 1,000 gallons of water from a well
Milk thirty cows
Heat five gallons of water
Grind 200 bushels of grain
Run a tool grinder for four hours
Shell thirty bushels of corn
Cool ten gallons of milk?

## Robbery at Gascosage

■ An April 16, 1951, newspaper article revealed the Gascosage REA office in Dixon had been broken into. Entry was made through a rear door at the office and though they suspected the burglar had only been looking for money, one object was taken. The article didn't reveal the nature of that object, only that it was found near the scene the next day. The office burglary followed a rash of recent petty thefts including about $50 of equipment taken off one truck. Contractors also reported having gas stolen from their trucks.

purchase price of approximately $210,000 included 60 miles of line serving approximately 1,500 new consumers, increasing the total to about 3,500 consumers on 750 miles of line. One of the main objectives of the transfer, which included the towns of Newburg, Dixon, Crocker, Jerome, Hancock, and Swedeborg, was to eliminate the wasteful duplication of lines in the area, to improve local service where possible, and to rebuild services where needed.

Only one community raised an eyebrow at the transfer of ownership. Crocker's board of alderman met to decide whether or not they should approve Gascosage's purchase of the Sho-Me system, wishing instead to leave it up to the consumers. A few citizens opposed the purchase since it would mean they would have to pay $5 to become a member of Gascosage Electric Cooperative. When the Missouri Public Service Commission granted its approval, Luther Riddle reported, "The first step in arranging for the sale is to contact users and ask them to sign in favor of the move." The sale, including the system in Crocker, ultimately took place during 1952.

By the time the September 28, 1954, annual meeting rolled around, the cooperative was able to report the best twelve months in its eight-year history. More than four hundred persons attended and waited to hear their names called for prizes that ranged from table lamps, to a bag of flour from

Joseph B. Lischwe, an original incorporator of Gascosage, speaks at the 1955 annual meeting.

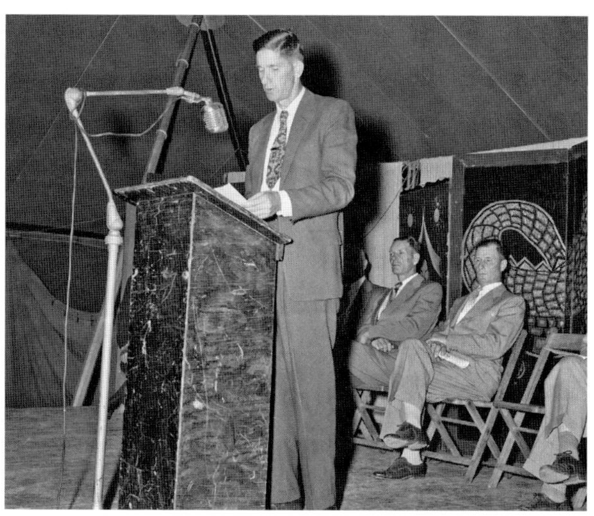

Director Carl Turner takes the podium under the tent in 1955.

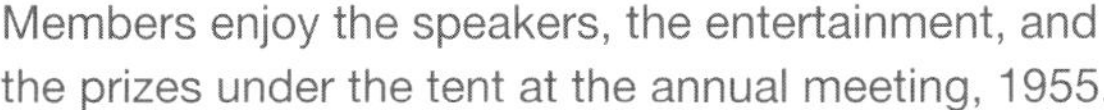

Members enjoy the speakers, the entertainment, and the prizes under the tent at the annual meeting, 1955.

The Ozark Playboys were a favorite at annual meetings.

Modern Food Store, to barbeque dinners from Mitchell's Café. Each attendee received a roll of aluminum foil from Kaiser Aluminum. The traveling caravan of the Missouri State REA once again provided the tents, chairs, and entertainment.

Pictured are Directors Euell Penland of Crocker, Carl Turner of Newburg, Adam Copeland of Dixon, Sherman Denton of Iberia, Joe Lischwe of Brinktown, Leonard Keeth of Iberia, Ferrel Roam of Richland, Fred McDonald of Iberia, and Manager Luther Riddle.

The co-op was then serving 4,224 members with 838.5 miles of line with an average of 5 meters per line. Their gross income for the previous year was $263,015 with operating costs of $252,962. "One reason for our good year was increased use of power for air conditioners in the cities," Luther Riddle announced. "The fact that our lines are well concentrated is bound to result in lower maintenance costs over the years." Loans from the REA totaled $1,702,203 with $96,830 in principal having been paid to that point and the plant was valued at $1,505,417.

In his opening remarks, Board President Joseph Lischwe reflected on the co-op's origins: "What happened," he said, "is that we kinda' got what the others left. At one time the plans were for other cooperatives to serve the area. Then it was decided that perhaps another group, which turned out to be ours, could do the job better. Now we are a good little co-op doing a good little job." ■

Working on the lines required teamwork. O the ground are Howar Goodman and Gene Allen with Pete Pemberton and Earl Prater on the pole.

CHAPTER FOUR

# Going Strong

■ Whatever success the program of rural cooperatives experienced, none of it would have been possible without the men who built and maintained the lines. While it's true that most of the world now takes electricity for granted, it's also true that those who helped make it possible will never forget what it took to get it.

## The Gascosage Linemen

Holes to set the poles were dug by hand using shovels and crowbars. Shovels with twelve-foot-long handles, dubbed a "banjo and spoon," were used in tandem to dig the hole. The banjo was a straight shovel used to pry the dirt loose from the sides of the hole. The end of the "spoon" had a bowl like a dipper that was used to bring the dirt up out of the hole after the "banjo" was used to fill it. When the rocky soil of the Gascosage area proved too much for the shovels, which it often did, dynamite got the job done. Gene Allen, who started work at Gascosage on the right-of-way crew in 1952, recalled his first experience with dynamite. "I was on the tie line from Doolittle to the Newburg Substation. They dumped me out over there and gave me a banjo and a spoon, a digging bar, a short-handled shovel, a shooting cord, dynamite and caps. I was seventeen years old and I was scared to death." The foreman came by a while later and, discovering that Gene had been reticent to try his hand at dynamite, taught him the ropes. "He showed me how to load the dynamite and about how much to use, how to tie it on the cord and use a flashlight battery to set it off. Once he showed me, I caught on pretty quick."

Getting the hole dug was just the beginning, though. Poles were set using an A-frame that went on the back of the truck with a cable running up it to set the pole. Sometimes a pole gin was used—two legs set in a "V" with a large-tooth metal bar between them for gripping the pole. "We would hoist the pole up as high as we could get it," Gene recalled, "one person would set the gin in place to hold the pole and then we'd walk down and get another hold on the pole and raise it up a little higher."

Gascosage linemen, including Luther Riddle in the top photo, are putting up the tent for the annual meeting at the new headquarters.

## Three Generations

■ Gene Allen and his father Henry went to work for Gascosage the same day—May 1, 1952. Using simple crosscut saws, they went to work for $1 an hour clearing right-of-way for the new lines. Later, they used a two-man Maul chain saw with one man running the motor while the other guided the end of the blade. The right-of-way crew was cutting out a swatch for the tie line from Doolittle to the Newburg Substation and, for a while, Gene worked with the construction crew and took a liking to it. When he approached Luther Riddle about moving to the construction crew, Luther said, "Gene, these boys on the construction truck all started at 85¢ an hour. I don't think it would be right to hire you at $1 an hour." Gene agreed to take his 15¢ an hour pay cut in exchange for the permanence of the construction crew and the benefits he would earn in the future.

Working his way up the ranks, Gene retired in 1999 from the job his son Mike now does—maintenance for the western district. Henry retired in 1966 and Gene treasures the time he spent working with his father and riding to and from work with him just as his own son Mike treasures everything he learned from his father going on calls with him. "We worked hard," Gene said, "but we made it enjoyable. Gascosage is one of the most wonderful experiences of my life. It's like a family to me. We worked hard, we played hard, and we all got along good."

When it was time to string the line, the crew's best friend was any local farmer with a horse or mule that could be put to work pulling the line the mile or so between poles.

Gascosage's outside employees, late 1950s.

Before bucket trucks came along, it wasn't unusual for a lineman to spend eight hours a day on a pole coming down only for lunch. The groundsman used a hand line to send up whatever the lineman needed. Absolutely essential were a good pair of boots with a strong arch support and a set of sharp gaff hooks that strapped on under the knee and at the ankle. Even still, the early gaff hooks didn't guarantee you'd stay up on the pole. "Back then, you had to learn to keep your knees out," said retired lineman Gene Allen. "If you put your knees up to the pole, your gaffs would kick out and down you'd come," collecting large jagged splinters along the way that had to be cut out.

Mr. Blaylock, AMEC safety instructor, presents safe driving awards to Gene Allen, Howard Goodman, Clint Bays, Bill Woody, Eugene Goodman, Luther Riddle, Charles Sooter, and Ray Clark, 1958.

Outside employees' safety meeting, 1958. Front row: Manager Luther A. Riddle, Leslie Jenkins, AMEC Safety Instructor Mr. Blaylock, and Clarence Parker. Standing: Eugene Goodman, Orville Griffin, Orville Pemberton, Charles Sooter, Clint Bays, James Williams, Howard Goodman, Raymond Clark, Henry Allen, Earl Prater, Bill Davis, Bill Woody, and Gene Allen.

Those early linemen came right off the farm and learned their jobs from the few men who preceded them and they all started, quite literally, at the bottom and worked their way up. As for safety, Gascosage provided them with hard hats and rubber gloves, even back then. "We very seldom wore them," Gene said. "There was just no ruling that made us wear them."

## The New Office

In mid-1956, Gascosage moved into its new and present home on Ellen Street, or Highway 28, dedicating the building on September 18. For the next few years, annual meetings were held under the tent on the grounds adjacent to the building. The conference room with its well-appointed kitchen has seen many Christmas celebrations and retirement parties and, as part of Gascosage's service to the community, has hosted many community organizations' meetings and events. When the 4-H club held a demonstration in the conference room of the new office on using an electric skillet to make pizza from a mix and bake cookies, 150 people attended.

The new headquarters of Gascosage Electric Cooperative.

RIGHT: Board President Joseph Lischwe (left) and Manager Luther Riddle (right) observe as REA Administrator David Hamil cuts the ribbon to dedicate the new headquarters on September 18, 1956.

BELOW: Norma (Veasman) Riddle, Jean Prater, Roma Lea Ray, and Berniece Bullock visit with David Hamil, REA administrator, at the dedication of the new office building.

## Building Lines, Building the Load

Every cooperative's obligation, by definition, is to provide service to *all* its members efficiently and at the lowest cost possible. For an electric cooperative, that means a constant and never-ending juggling act between building lines and then loading them up to help share the cost. By 1959, the juggling act was well underway for Gascosage. Articles in the *Gascosage News* featured members' testimonies on the ways in which electricity was making their home and farm life easier and more efficient. The advantages of electric heat with its clean, even heat and comfortable humidity was a frequent topic. Luther Riddle announced the formation of a power use department with one employee dedicated to advising and educating consumers on living with electricity.

Clint Bays managed to operate the new radio system despite the bulky Hercules gloves.

Of course, "building the load" meant they had to ensure the reliability of the service. During the summer of 1959, Gascosage linemen hung voltage recorders on lines throughout the system to measure voltage. A study revealed low voltage in certain areas where the 7,200-volt lines, more than adequate when originally installed, were facing unanticipated demands. Voltage regulators were installed to increase efficiency and protect appliances. Luther proudly announced, "Consumers should notice that their television pictures no longer shrink and their lights don't dim when a large appliance kicks on."

Many of those attending the 1959 annual meeting were among the cooperative's first consumers.

The co-op also installed mobile radio units in each of its trucks. Linemen could now go from one service call to the next without returning to the office, and materials and equipment were quickly dispatched to the trouble spot, dramatically decreasing response time and speeding up customer service.

The 1959 annual meeting was postponed until October 22 to allow time for the new Dixon High School to be completed as the meeting's new site. The gymnasium provided seating that made it possible for everyone to see and hear better than at the outdoor meetings. Entertainment was provided by the Country Gentlemen and Shug Fisher, stars of the ABC Television Network show *Jubilee USA*, and the Dixon Youth Recreation Association prepared the noon meal as a fundraiser. Manager Luther Riddle announced that Gascosage had recently received approval of a $370,000 loan for system upgrades and the construction of 30 miles of distribution lines to bring electric service to 450 new members.

Gascosage linemen. Front: Bill Davis, Howard Goodman, and Les Jenkins. Standing: Jim Williams, Eugene Goodman, Bill Woody, and Ray Clark. Top: Gene Allen.

## Protecting the Co-op's Future

Ironically, though some would say predictably, the very investor-owned utility companies that declined to provide power to the rural areas later undermined both the integrity and the stability of the rural electric cooperatives.

In the late 1950s, Sho-Me and other managers from regional generation and transmission cooperatives started to discuss the possibility of a statewide G & T. Luther Riddle was quoted saying, "Twenty-five years ago the electrical utility industry failed to recognize the farmer as a producer as well as a consumer. Because of this, they made their first mistake in failing to extend their distribution lines into rural areas. In more recent years, the same utility industry has failed to make power available on a wholesale basis to the load centers of the electric cooperatives except on conditions which imposed crippling conditions unacceptable to the cooperatives."

1960 Gascosage Board of Directors. Front: Carl Durtschi and Joe Lischwe. Second row: Dorsey Willis, Euell Penland, and Raymond Kloeppel. Third row: Leonard Keeth, Harold Hamilton, Robert Law, and Carl Turner.

Members register for the annual meeting in the early 1960s...

.....and crowd the Dixon High School gymnasium to hear the status of their cooperative.

Afterward they enjoy a free lunch on the high school grounds.

Finally, on February 6, 1961, fifteen incorporators, Luther Riddle among them, signed the articles of incorporation to create Associated Electric Cooperative, Inc. "Associated would become the vehicle for pooling the cooperatives' resources," Luther explained, "and building the facilities required for greater use of the Bull Shoals and Table Rock hydropower by Missouri cooperatives."

When the Department of the Interior granted final approval on July 25, 1962, Associated became the primary source for the generation and procurement of power for Missouri cooperatives and, for Gascosage, Sho-Me's primary responsibility shifted to that of transmission creating the three-tier system that exists today.

Luther explained, "In 1962, after an extended period of negotiations, the Missouri G & Ts pooled their generating plants and transmission lines through the newly formed Associated Electric Cooperative to provide power on a uniform basis to the total load requirement of the electric cooperatives. In this arrangement, the G & T's have retained their operating identity and thus kept control close to the grass roots."

Luther took numerous opportunities to defend Gascosage and the cooperative concept in general, urging the members to participate fully in their cooperative's operation. At various times, the anti-cooperative propaganda claimed co-ops operated tax-free using taxpayer dollars. In response, REA-financed cooperatives made a point of distinguishing themselves from the financing body that made them possible, and publicly revealed the amount of taxes they paid. "Your Cooperative and the REA are not the same thing," the ads said.

Finally, in 1960 the National Rural Electric Cooperative Association (NRECA) began a public relations campaign called, "Tell the Nation the Truth" or "TNT." It was a national advertising campaign aimed at combating the negative advertising that was being bankrolled by the investor-owned power companies who were portraying the cooperatives as socialist, un-American, even a communist plot. Only ten years had passed since Senator Joe McCarthy's witch hunt for communists within the media and entertainment business turned the country upside down, and America's Cold War with the Soviet Union was still going strong.

In another sign of the times, Gascosage Office Manager Charles Ellis was given the task of representing the co-op on the Maries and Pulaski Counties civil defense information committees. It

Iberia consumer and turkey farmer John Jarret (left) visits with Gascosage employee Charles Sooter. *Photo courtesy of* Rural Electric Missourian.

was a rational response to the Cold War threat of attack that, in retrospect, seems somewhat irrational though it indeed swept the nation. Their job was to inform rural families of the radiation threat and defenses against it, to induce them to prepare family shelters, and take measures to protect their livestock and feed supplies. Though it diminished in fervor over the years, the NRECA's "Tell the Nation the Truth" campaign wasn't discontinued until 1994.

## Moving On

Occasionally, system upgrades extended to the office equipment as well. From the beginning people who lived outside the towns read their own meters and referred to a rate book to figure out their bills. Then in 1964, a modern Addressograph machine was purchased to replace the tedious process of keeping all the accounts by hand. That was about the time Gayle Prater started working at the co-op and recalled the Addressograph machine. "There was a plate for each member with all the information," she explained. "You had to take the plate out to record each customer's billing. Every year we had to run them off and put a book together—thirteen pages to put in every book on

Bill Davis at the dispatch microphone, circa 1960. Bill retired in 1991 and was awarded the A. C. Burrows Award in 1995.

Jim Williams, Orville Griffin, and Clint Bays, early 1960s.

Bill Davis, Steve Benton, and Clarence Parker showing off a new truck.

Earl Prater, who would later become operations manager, is reading meters in the early 1960s.

All-electric “Gold Medallion” homes became the rage in the early 1960s.

## Capital Credit Bonanza

■ When Gascosage issued capital credit checks at the 1964 annual meeting, Luther Riddle wrote in his regular column on the many ways people told him the money would be used. One storekeeper told him of the pleasure he experienced watching senior citizens, who normally only purchased necessities, using their checks for small luxuries. A mother of three told him the capital credits check meant her children would get new coats, slacks, and overshoes while yet another mother used it to surprise her children by getting them exactly what they wanted for Christmas. In one local community, the city clerk was relieved to see the check since it meant they could now cover unexpected expenses not provided for in the budget. As one local businessman remarked, the actual amount of money refunded was multiplied many times over, in terms of buying power and benefit to business and individuals, as it circulated throughout the area.

Even better than the light bulbs was the capital credit checks they received for the first time in 1964.

every consumer and get them all out by January first." As archaic as it sounds compared to today's electronic systems, the Addressograph made billing procedures much easier for the office staff and reduced the errors that occurred when numbers had to be transferred by hand.

Attendance at the eighteenth annual meeting in November of 1964 reached three thousand people, all of whom enjoyed a free lunch after standing in line to receive their capital credit check, a "first" for both. The following spring Gascosage announced a new substation was being put into operation near Dixon to replace the older, smaller one that was now overloaded by the demand. As a result, Gascosage was able to bring full capacity service to all the members who were on lines fed out of Dixon. ■

Members line up to register and receive their free light bulbs at the 1964 annual meeting.

---

**Source:**

Holt, Russ. *Win-Win: An Informal History of Associated Electric Cooperative, Inc.* Associated Electric Cooperative, Inc. 1969.

The new substation a
Frank's Switch covere
7.5 acres located 4
miles east of Dixon.
At the 1973 dedicatio
are David Hamil, REA
administrator; Jerry
Diddle, manager of
Associated Electric;
unknown; Gascosage
Manager Luther
Riddle; and Charles
Boulson, manager of
Sho-Me Power.

CHAPTER FIVE

# Politics and Power Supply

By the 1960s, the spirit of unity that bolstered the American people through the post World War II years had dimmed somewhat. It was replaced with sharply defined ideological differences that were beginning to shape the political landscape impacting issues that reached even as far as the country's rural electric cooperatives.

When President Lyndon Johnson appeared at the twenty-sixth annual meeting of the National Rural Electric Cooperative Association in February of 1968, he and other speakers warned those in attendance of the urban/rural crisis. With floods of people moving from the cities to rural areas, he cautioned them to protect their cooperatives from attack by those who did not understand the cooperative system and what it took to build it.

The 1966 winners of the Youth Tour essay contest from Gascosage were Randy Hoops of Crocker, Jerel Kerby of Newburg, Marshall Miller of Dixon, and Gary Wall of Iberia with Manager Luther Riddle (center).

Members line up for capital credit checks and a free lunch at the 1967 annual meeting.

"It isn't enough to say that the lights will never go out again in the countryside," Johnson said. "It isn't time to stand pat and be satisfied with the status quo—not when your battles are America's battles—not when your struggles for a better rural life can mean better cities, better suburbs, a better future for every American. I will do all in my power to work with you, to help you, to encourage you. I will support your right of your systems to territorial integrity—to continue serving the areas where you pioneered."

## A Political Storm

The administration of Richard Nixon proved less friendly to the REA and its co-ops. When Congress failed to make enough loan funds available to the REA to meet the growing demand in 1969, the co-ops were forced to form the National Rural Utilities Cooperative Finance Corporation, more commonly referred to as the CFC.

The part that no one ever sees is all the paperwork that precedes the annual meeting. Pictured here are Jean Prater, Gayle Prater, Ethel May Allen, Vicki DeVault, and Lou Manes.

Then, on December 29, 1972, a day the REA would dub "Black Friday," the Nixon administration announced the termination of the REA loan program. The Department of Agriculture issued a press release saying that future loans would no longer be made under the Rural Electrification Act but instead under a new Rural Development Act, HB 12931 signed into law on August 30, 1972. President Nixon called for revisions to the REA loan process, among them a reduction in the subsidy that was inherent in the 2 percent loans that fell below the interest rate normally charged for government loans. "I was working for REA at that time," John Greenlee recalled. "My wife and I were in Topeka, Kansas visiting a friend for Christmas when it popped up on the news. What a shock—not knowing if I still had a job."

Rallying a grass roots effort of protest, 1,400 representatives from rural electric cooperatives flocked to Washington in late January 1973 to protest Nixon's action. "It gave us a lot of political clout," John recalled. "People were upset and they let their voices be heard." They returned again in May to urge Congress to pass new legislation that would restore the REA, which it did by an overwhelming margin. President Nixon signed the bill that expanded financial resources available to both rural electric and telephone cooperatives into law on May 11, 1973, the thirty-eighth anniversary of the REA.

Manager Luther Riddle acknowledged members who'd attended every Gascosage annual meeting through the years. Shown are Joe Lischwe, Joe Newkirk, Leonard Keeth, Marion Matthews, Floyd Roark, Erma Matthews, and Dora Atwell.

## HB 1092

It was inevitable the increased commercial and residential business that came with the area's growth would catch the attention of the private power companies who had originally shunned the rural business opportunity. As a result, new lines began springing up in certain areas, built over and around existing lines at greater expense and danger than the original lines. The REA's rules required the rural cooperatives serve everyone in their area who requested service but were excluded from towns whose population exceeded three thousand except for members who were annexed into a city. Yet the private power companies had no such restrictions and were free to leapfrog existing lines to pick up profitable commercial accounts.

In 1972, Missouri's rural electric cooperatives banded together, taking their grievances to the Public Service Commission (PSC). Co-op representatives served on a special legislative committee meeting

A study in contrasts: Laymond Humphrey of Dixon uses electricity to pump air into the tires of a horse drawn wagon at Hayes' Standard Station, 1969. *Photo courtesy of Catherine Hayes.*

with state legislators. HB 1092 was introduced which was intended to assign territories for all power suppliers to guard against the unsightly and hazardous duplication of lines.

The private power companies argued before the Public Service Commission it was, in fact, the rural cooperatives that were encroaching on their territory. Powerless to do anything, the PSC's only response was it would take a legislative act to resolve the dilemma and, ultimately, passage of the bill was never secured.

The Gascosage Board of Directors, 1971. Seated: Joseph Lischwe, Carl Durtschi, Euell Penland, Dorsey Willis, and Raymond Kloeppel. Standing: Carl Turner, Leonard Keeth, Manager Luther Riddle, Harold Hamilton, and Robert Law.

In 1974, another statewide committee was formed to address the issue. A bill came before the Missouri legislature that would place rural electric cooperatives under the jurisdiction of the Missouri Public Service Commission, Missouri being one of only eleven states that did not regulate rural cooperatives. The duplication of lines made it possible for disgruntled or dishonest customers to simply switch their service from one company to another, leaving the power providers to bear the cost of switching out meters. Governor Joe Teasdale signed the legislation the committee ultimately proposed, which didn't provide territorial protection, but ended the practice of switching power providers.

Among the many community organizations hosted at the Gascosage building is the board meeting for Dixon Manor Senior Center, 1973.

The issue was brought to Gascosage's back door when in April of 1973 the co-op's franchise with the city of Dixon expired. The next month, city officials considered placing a referendum on the ballot to let citizens decide whether or not to move to a municipal electric system. Newburg had already switched to a municipal system back in 1968. The *Dixon Pilot* interviewed Luther Riddle with Alderman Jimmy Meaders to present the facts. When asked if Gascosage would vacate the area entirely if Dixon went to a municipal system, Luther emphatically answered, "No." He added, "When electricity first came to this area, we brought it here. I had to borrow a chair to sit on in my office and I had a home-made table to work on. I still have that table stored away as a reminder of what it takes to establish an excellent electric system from scratch. You don't just hire men to string wire, hook up all the equipment and turn on the current."

Committed to preserving the integrity of the co-op, Luther Riddle attended their meetings, presenting facts and figures to inform them and the public on the costs involved with start-up, maintenance, materials, and labor. He explained the wholesale cost of power was much lower for the cooperative than it would be for a municipality, particularly given the reliability of power that Gascosage offered the consumers. If the state legislation had passed as written, it would have eliminated duplication of services by two electric power suppliers in the same territory.

To help them understand the scope of their undertaking, Luther reported the co-op was now operating on some $2 million of borrowed money, some of which was now costing them as much as 8 percent interest. His point was to illustrate the amount of money the city would have to borrow to start up a system and the difficulty in obtaining those funds. Also, who would operate and maintain it? “We can work together and solve our problems,” he said, “but we can’t remain at each other’s throats and get anything done.” Ultimately, the citizens of Dixon voted to renew the franchise but the delay cost the city almost $14,000 in lost revenue for the two-year period plus the cost of the feasibility study.

## Promoting Electric Appliances

■ In 1968, Gascosage began a program whereby members could purchase appliances through the co-op and have them installed free. Mr. and Mrs. M. J. Foley of Route 1, Dixon were among the first Gascosage members to take advantage of it and reported being pleased with the promptness and neatness of the co-op employee who installed their new hot water heater. They had previously received an AM-FM radio with the purchase of an electric range. The Foleys were asked to represent the co-op on its monthly television show and Mrs. Foley appeared with Lloyd Evans on the *Man with a Mike* show on Channel 3 out of Springfield.

The fact that Gascosage had long ago decided to be an involved member of the community might have helped in situations such as this. As early as 1966, the co-op began helping the Dixon,

The first 4-H group to meet at the new headquarters enjoyed a demonstration on cooking with electric skillets.

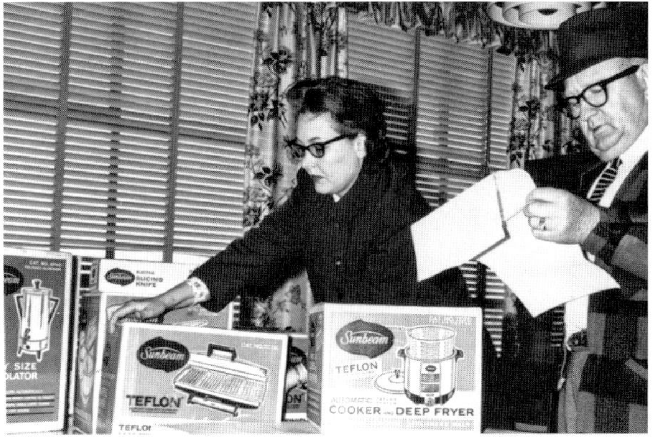


Jean Prater and Edwin (Birdie) Russell (who owned a Sears appliance store in Dixon) inventory appliances purchased by Gascosage Electric Cooperative for area high school home economics classes, 1967.

Crocker, and Iberia High Schools home economics classes by providing electric appliances. Having been approached by the schools, Luther assigned his office manager, Jean Prater, to visit the schools and take an inventory to determine their needs. The co-op then purchased the small and large appliances at a volume discount and then sold the used appliances at the end of each term. Local folks watched for the appliance sale at the co-op. "We had appliances sitting in the lobby, the conference room, all over the place," Jean recalled.

## Stepping up for the Linemen

Finally, it was time for the linemen to be on the receiving end of upgrades. In 1964, Gascosage got their first hydraulic boom truck for raising poles. Unlike the A-frame apparatus, the boom truck revolved from side to side, eliminating the need to position the truck at precisely the right angle for raising the pole. A new cab and chassis were purchased and Gene Allen took it to St. Louis to McKay Power where the boom was installed and, once back at Gascosage, the bed from the old truck was installed.

The Gascosage linemen.

It would be a few years before bucket trucks came along to cut down on the time linemen spent climbing poles. In the meantime, a fiberglass extension fitted on the end of the boom was a good compromise. One man had to operate the boom while the other was in the basket working on the line, unlike the bucket trucks where the man in the bucket has the controls. The basket,

### Jean and Earl Prater

■ Of all Gascosage's dedicated employees, two were not only married to their work but to each other as well—Jean and Earl Prater. Jean moved to Dixon with her parents in 1945 and went to work for Gascosage on September 20, 1950. Moving her way up through the ranks, Jean became office manager in August of 1987 and in 1991 received the A. C. Burrows Service Award from the Association of Missouri Electric Cooperatives. Earl's family moved to Dixon in 1942 and he started with Gascosage in 1953 first staking lines, then as a lineman, and then for twenty-one years as the area service foreman for the eastern half of Gascosage's territory before becoming manager of operations. During the 1987 ice storm then-manager Jerry Williams commented, "If it weren't for Earl, things wouldn't have run so smooth. He knew where everyone lived and sent workmen right where they were supposed to be."

and even the newer bucket trucks, didn't put an end to climbing poles, however. To this day, maintenance crews work singularly and climb virtually every pole they work on. Nonetheless, it was a big improvement.

In 1973 Gascosage finally got their first digger truck, primarily because of OSHA regulations that prevented them from carrying both caps and dynamite on the same vehicle. Since Gascosage crews normally worked with one truck, a digger truck became a necessity.

Regulations, however, are not always enough to raise awareness where safety is concerned, but the message came home to Gascosage when a tragic accident occurred in 1975. Line foreman Clarence Parker lost his left arm and left leg below the knee when the line he believed had been de-energized proved to be hot as a result of some undiscovered crossphasing outside the substation. Clarence survived the accident and from then on, greater attention was paid to wearing safety gear and following safety guidelines.

TOP: A safety meeting in the Gascosage conference room in June of 1972.

BOTTOM: Clint Bays, Charlie Sooter, Myrel Dake, Jim Williams, Ray Clark, and Earl Prater accept their safety award in March of 1973.

## Operation Peak Alert

In 1971, Associated made plans to build a new generating unit with a capacity of approximately 600 kilowatts plus related transmission facilities in order to keep up with the increasing demand for power.

Unlike the early years when peak usage meant the evening milking of cows, peak usage now meant a significantly increased population arriving home from work or school and simultaneously turning on televisions, radios, washing machines, dryers, and stoves. Late in 1976 the Association of Missouri Electric Cooperatives (AMEC) launched a statewide program called Operation Peak Alert to ensure the most efficient and economical use of existing generation and transmission equipment. Members were urged to curtail usage during emergencies to avoid the high cost of purchasing supplemental power.

Bill Davis takes direction from Ethel May Allen as he prepares to place the star atop the Gascosage Christmas tree, 1972.

## Blackout

■ At 8:15 in the morning of February 21, 1974, all current in the entire Gascosage service area ceased to function. The blackout was caused when a transformer from Sho-Me Power Corporation to Gascosage failed. Checkout personnel in grocery stores were forced to turn the cranks on their cash registers by hand in order to tally up sales. Restaurants had to cook without the use of their ventilating fans, stores were left in total darkness, and gas stations lost the use of their electrically driven gas pumps. The local post office was forced to cancel thousands of pieces of mail by hand and at least one hog farmer reported that his animals ran right through a fence that normally carried electric current and went AWOL. Because the likelihood of such a breakdown ever occurring was so small, Gascosage did not have a spare transformer on hand. The lights went back on at exactly 1:25 p.m.—not bad considering the enormous electric transformer had to be transported to the Pisgah area of Dixon from Marshfield, Missouri, some seventy-five miles away.

The truck used to spray for right-of-way clearing.

Operation Peak Alert was first tested as a result of record cold temperatures on New Year's Eve 1976. Associated Electric Cooperative in Springfield, which monitored the statewide REC system, saw the electrical demand rapidly increasing the afternoon of December 30. When it became apparent the peak was going even higher on December 31, Operation Peak Alert was put into effect; pre-arranged TV and radio announcements were broadcast asking REC members to stagger or delay the use of some of their electric appliances. In just a few hours, the demand began leveling and then dropping as 356,000 rural electric cooperative members voluntarily reduced their demand by an estimated 50,000 kilowatts. In July 1977 when the Newburg and Crocker Substations recorded record usage during a heat wave, members again responded well to the peak alert system.

Because power suppliers had to have generating capacity adequate to meet peak demand, a "ratchet clause" allowed them to pass the costs they incurred in providing additional power to the distributing cooperative, which then imposed a power cost adjustment to the members. The resulting demand charge then remained, over and above what was actually used, until a higher peak demand was established.

Complicating things even further, the United Mine Workers of America launched a national coal strike in December of 1977, forcing Missouri rural electric cooperatives to purchase higher cost power generated by oil and gas plants in states in the South and West. Co-op members across the state were urged to decrease their use of this more expensive power from the oil and gas-fired plants. Fortunately, the strike ended in March of 1978 and though the additional cost for each cooperative member amounted to 1.5¢ cents/kWh, an average of $15 per month per member, rural electric cooperative officials across the state opted to delay passing on the increased cost to their members.

The days of "load building" and "use more, pay less" were about to come to an end. One co-op's report in 1975 showed that 48.5¢ of every dollar going out was put toward the purchase of power. By 1976 the cost of wholesale power had increased nearly 100 percent over the cost of purchased power in 1970.

Throughout the seventies, the nation was faced with increasing energy costs, resulting in increased construction costs and higher interest rates. Government regulations helped to increase the cost of wholesale power but rather than institute permanent rate increases, most cooperative's boards chose instead to apply PCAs (power cost adjustments) to the members' bill as a separate expense in order to meet the cooperative's obligations.

Vivian Thompson, Ethel May Allen, Francis Hoffman, Pat Williams, Gayle Prater, Jean Prater, and Janet Rigsby in 1980.

In January of 1977, Gascosage Electric Cooperative was notified by its power supplier that its wholesale power costs would be increased 2.42 mills/kWh, which equated to approximately $137,000 for the same amount of power purchased in 1976. Sho-Me Power was passing along rate hikes they received from Associated Electric Cooperative who generated the power for the RECs in Missouri. They cited the rising cost of coal and materials used for generating electricity, plant equipment costs, and inflation as the reasons for the increase.

According to the Handy-Whitman, Inc. Index, the construction costs of steam generating plants increased by 66.5 percent in the previous five years; transmission construction costs were up 72.1 percent, and distribution construction climbed 66.7 percent between July 1, 1971 and July 1976. In the same five-year period, equipment cost increases at Gascosage included the following:

- Treated pine poles went up 166.7 percent
- Cross arms went up 144.7 percent
- Distribution conductors went up 88 percent
- Overhead transmission conductors went up 87.4 percent
- Mercury luminaries with standards went up 108 percent

The same amount of kilowatt-hours of electricity purchased in 1976 cost Gascosage $191,007 more than the year before. Said Manager Luther Riddle, "A new rate increase will be needed and will go into effect March 1, 1977. We're hoping that costs will begin to level off, but we can see no end to increased costs at this time." ■

Jim Clark hangs a capacitor bank from the bucket.

CHAPTER SIX

# Endings and Beginnings

■ Luther Riddle dedicated most of his life to Gascosage Electric Cooperative and his success was acknowledged during the fiftieth anniversary celebration of rural electric cooperatives in Missouri when he was presented with the Rural Electric Pioneer Award. At the Association of Missouri Electric Cooperatives' annual meeting at the Lodge of the Four Seasons on November 8, 1985, he was again acknowledged and presented with the Distinguished Service Award. The award was given "in recognition of Mr. Riddle's outstanding accomplishments and service to electric cooperatives and for contributions above and beyond normal duty in furthering state and national effects on the principles and progress of rural electrification."

Luther had, in fact, dedicated his life to both Gascosage Electric Cooperative and the cooperative system in general. By this time, however, his health was beginning to fail and despite his refusal to give in to physical limitations, Luther finally accepted the board's urging that he retire. He turned seventy-six in January of 1987 and retired the following June from a position he'd held since 1946. He was honored at a retirement dinner held at the Ramada Inn in Waynesville where approximately 116 guests were present to pay tribute. By all accounts, Luther was a demanding manager, though he never asked more of his employees than he was willing to ask of himself. During his forty-one years as manager, he held the astounding record of having never missed a board meeting during his tenure. Though, as he embarked on his retirement, he himself paid tribute to the employees of whom he'd asked so much. "We have had very dedicated employees throughout the years," he said. "We've been very lucky to have this kind of people working for us." Sadly, Luther Riddle passed away on April 11, 1988.

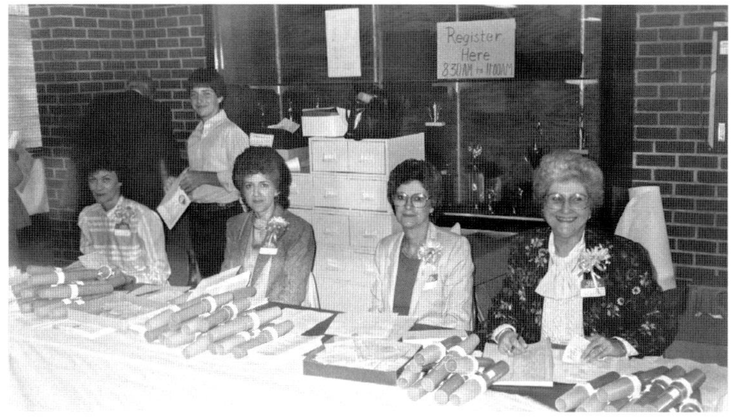

Gayle Prater, Janet Rigsby, Vivian Thompson, and Pat Williams await the members' arrival at the 1985 annual meeting.

For the next few months following Luther's retirement, Jean Prater stepped in as acting manager while the board conducted their search for his replacement. The following October, Jerry Williams was hired to succeed Luther as manager. Jerry's experience with cooperatives began while he was still in college when he had an opportunity to learn all aspects of the business at Central Rural Cooperative in Stillwater. Following college, he worked at Choctaw Electric Cooperative. His primary concern as he took over the helm at Gascosage was the increasing cost of wholesale power and the rising concerns over peak demand. "Generating facilities are required to be built to handle the largest load at any given time," he said. "If we can shift some usage off the peak times, we can defer building generating plants for several years."

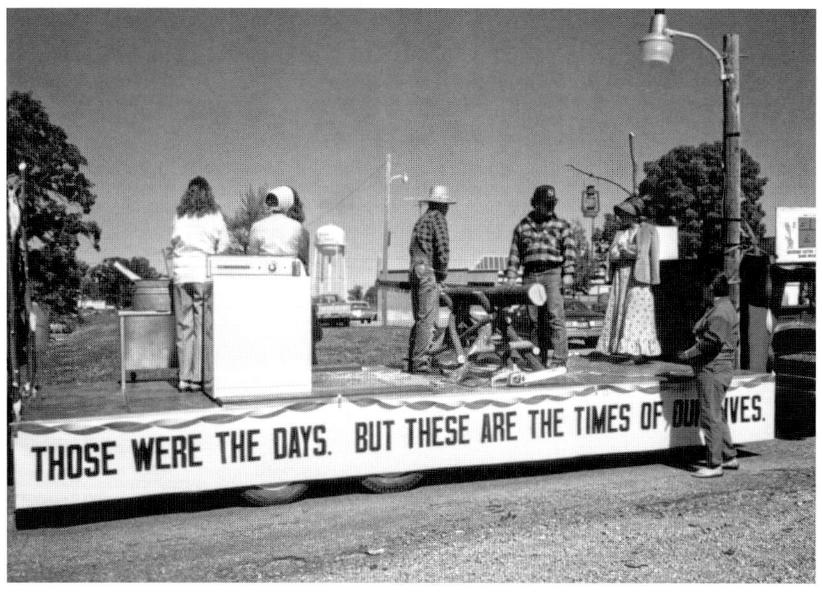

THOSE WERE THE DAYS. BUT THESE ARE THE TIMES OF

Gascosage's float in the 1987 Cow Days Parade.

Just three months after his hire, however, Mother Nature got his attention when icy rains hit the area on Christmas Day. Crews from Gascosage were called out just after noon. Jean Prater recalled, "About half of our system was affected. The worst hit areas included Swedeborg, Crocker, Richland, Iberia and Dixon. All of our employees both in the office and in the field worked around the clock Christmas night."

The Gascosage team, 1985. Kneeling: Mike Allen, Herb Colley, Myrel Dake, Ralph Withers, Craig Rivera, and Karl Brandt. Standing: Luther Riddle, Bill Davis, Larry Prater, Ray Clark, Gene Allen, Bill Thompson, Harold Zepp, Earl Prater, Jim Clark, Jean Prater, Gayle Prater, Frances Huffman, Ethel May Allen, Janet Rigsby, Vivian Thompson, and Pat Williams.

The next day emergency crews from Ralls County Cooperative in New London, Cuivre River Cooperative from Troy, and Three Rivers Cooperative at Linn were called in. After forty-eight hours, the major lines had been restored. Local fire departments, telephone company, and police departments pitched in to help. In several instances, lines heavy with ice fell and caused fires near or on homes. Fire trucks responded to eight calls during Christmas afternoon and night. Two big fires occurred in Jerome and Lebanon with one home being completely destroyed. Fire companies from Camdenton and Laclede Counties plus a water truck from Osage Beach assisted when a fire broke out in Lebanon's business district the morning after the storm destroying several businesses and causing smoke and water damage to others. Even the local television stations were knocked out for several days.

Tracey Cross of Dixon, Stephanie Tappe of Crocker, and Jared Buckley of Iberia were the winners of the 1989 Youth Tour.

Mike Allen commented, "People need to go on a storm in order to see what the employees go through. The 1987 storm was the worst the co-op had ever seen. The ice kept falling down around us. You'd think you were making headway and next thing you know, they'd call to tell you that the place you'd just left was back down." Earl Prater was operations manager at the time and, knowing what lines the men were working on, it was his job to call the crews and turn them around to go back to where they'd just been working.

What the storm exposed was the need to catch up with the pole change program and right-of-way maintenance. The majority of trees in the area were pines, which were particularly susceptible to breakage when weighted down with heavy snow or ice.

## Troubled Times

Over the next few years, Gascosage Electric Cooperative faced the challenge of serving its members with its usual efficiency in the midst of turmoil. No organization is immune to occasional disputes, but when opinions are sharply divided in an otherwise close-knit community of people, factions inevitably arise and long-standing friendships get caught in the crosshairs.

In early January of 1988, Gascosage's board of directors dismissed Manager Jerry Williams. On March 10, 1988, a group calling themselves Concerned Citizens for Justice published a letter to the board of directors protesting Williams's dismissal, citing among other things his involvement in the community as evidence of his commitment to Gascosage. Shortly thereafter, the board hired Elroy McMillian of Dixon to be Gascosage's new manager. McMillian previously served as vice president of construction for the Rajac Construction and Development Corporation. The following month, a petition drive emerged for the convening of a special membership meeting "for the purpose of removing the complete board of directors and electing a new board of directors, the current board members to be removed for failure to properly conduct the business of the cooperative, including firing the most recent manager without any notice or opportunity to correct any perceived deficiencies prior to such firing."

Manager Jerry Williams, 1987.

Carlene and Elroy McMillian, manager.

Those who disagreed with the board over the firing of Jerry Williams were now also critical of their hiring of McMillian, citing his lack of experience at working for an electrical cooperative. In one newspaper article, a member described the board's actions as "a coup with courtesy." A special public meeting was held to discuss a petition drive that could, if successful, have resulted in the removal of the entire board. Only one member of the board, Euell Penland of Crocker, attended and a handful of citizens attended in support of the board. Williams made it clear he had no intention of filing a lawsuit over his dismissal.

Amid the turmoil, life went on at Gascosage and when Manager Elroy McMillian attended the May 1988 meeting of the Consumer Electric

Harold Zepp, Gascosage bookkeeper.

Bill Davis works at the pole pile at the Gascosage office.

Power Association (CEPA), he reported on a move to restrict power generation at Truman Dam that Gascosage, among others, opposed. "Limitations have been placed on Truman Dam power generation because of possible environmental impacts downstream," he explained. "However, numerous studies have shown no unacceptable impacts in relation to soil erosion or fish spawning." Though there were signs of minor impacts such as soil erosion and downstream flooding in areas that had already been designated as flood plains, the many large benefits, in McMillian's opinion, far outweighed the minor impacts.

At the September 29 annual meeting, Harold Hamilton, president of the board of directors, presented Norma Riddle, accompanied by her children Luther Jr. and Lisa, with a plaque honoring the memory of her late husband. It was the largest annual meeting in twenty years with close to one thousand members attending. President Hamilton also praised the employees for their outstanding efforts during the December 1987 ice storm and reassured members there would be no rate increases. "Despite a $100,000 rate raise to us from our supplier," he said, "we still have as much money on hand as last year." At the time, Gascosage boasted 6,688 members and assets nearing $7 million. The Dixon High School Jazz Band and the Sounds of His Coming, a gospel group from Willow Springs, provided entertainment.

At the 1991 annual meeting, members of Gascosage voted, for the second year in a row, not to re-elect three incumbent board members. The campaigns were, at times, personal and hard-hitting. In response to some member complaints, the board opted to change the voting system in order to provide the members with more privacy. Instead of the casual system of voting previously used, members were asked to form lines to obtain their ballots and cast their votes, placing their ballots into a box.

The news was not all bad, however. McMillian reported the cooperative "was in good fiscal condition and operating within budget." They had accomplished a lot of right-of-way clearing,

## Remembering Luther Riddle

■ Luther Riddle, by all accounts, was an old-style manager, one who took the responsibilities bestowed upon him seriously and expected no less from those around him. Said Gayle Prater, "He was very strict, but we all did our jobs." Being human, the employees sometimes found occasion for relief from their daily workload. "Once in a while we goofed off when Mr. Riddle was at a meeting," Gayle recalled. "But even if we goofed off, we knew we had our work to do so we just worked twice as hard."

Though current board member Bill Davis described Luther as "a hard man to work for," he was not without a sense of humor. Bill worked in the office for many years but occasionally he was called to work outside. "We had a door in back, that after you pushed it up, it'd start creeping back down," Bill recalled. "I got in the line truck and started driving out. By that time it had come down about two feet and I tore the bottom section off it. Luther called the boys and told them I was on the way but I was bringing part of the door with me."

Along with his work ethic, Luther was known for his frugality. When Bill Thompson and Bill Davis worked together clearing right-of-way, Luther finally relented to their requests for a new chain saw. "He intended for us to get a Homelite, which was cheaper, but we hated them," Bill Thompson said. They returned with the more expensive Stihl saw and when Luther came in and saw the two Bill's, he asked them what they'd purchased. When they told him, Bill said Luther's only response was, "I was afraid of that!"

Pat Williams's job on the front desk put her in constant contact with the consumers who, from time to time, got a little belligerent. Pat recalled when that happened, Luther would come out and tell them, "The way this girl is telling you—that's how it is."

When people paid their bills late, Pat was under strict instructions from Luther to charge late fees with no exceptions, "even if my dad comes in," he said. One older gentleman, however, was having difficult times. When Luther asked Pat if she charged him late fees she said, "No, I just can't. I know he doesn't have much money and if I have to charge him a penalty, I'll pay it." Luther relented, saying, "No, that's all right."

Anyone who knows the burden that comes with big responsibilities knows how easy it is to be misunderstood from time to time. On more than one occasion, Gene Allen found himself "crashing heads" with Luther but out of mutual respect the two managed to work out their differences. "Luther was a good manager," Gene said. "He made the co-op what it was. He thought a lot of me and I thought the world and all of him. He was my bread and butter."

Members filled the Dixon High School Gymnasium in 1991.

converted lines from single-phase to three-phase, and all without raising rates or borrowing any additional money. At the time, Gascosage boasted the lowest rates of all forty-one distribution cooperatives in Missouri. Despite the fact that Sho-Me Power Corporation had just announced a 2–3 percent rate increase to become effective in January 1992, McMillian announced the cooperative would be able to absorb the increased cost without raising rates.

The Dixon High School Band entertained members before the beginning of the 1991 annual meeting.

Carl Turner of Doolittle, a former member of the GEC Board of Directors, entertained the crowd by appearing on stage with the Singing Disciples. JR's Kountry Kitchen provided the 1,697 people in attendance with 600 pounds of barbeque beef, 41 gallons of baked beans, and 210 pounds of coleslaw.

Once again, the cooperative faced turmoil when the board voted on January 21, 1992, to terminate Manager Elroy McMillian. The board appointed Director Charles Sease of Dixon as acting manager.

During the board's regular meeting in February, about fifty supporters of McMillian filled the front lobby of the co-op building. Current Board President Walt Weider fielded dozens of questions about the firing and a petition was circulated in the area asking the board to reconsider their firing of McMillian, a local man who had a measure of support from some of the members.

At that year's annual meeting, two proposals were brought forward for the membership's vote. Recent population growth in the portion of Phelps County served by Gascosage resulted in unequal representation based on the number of consumers served. The proposal was to shift one board spot from Miller County to Phelps giving two each in Miller, Maries, and Phelps Counties and three from Pulaski County. The proposal was overwhelmingly approved. The second proposal, which only received token opposition in a voice vote, amended the bylaws to include a statement forbidding any future written employment contracts requiring the cooperative to pay any amount as severance pay unless such contract shall have been specifically authorized by a vote of the members.

Three new board members—Jim Humphrey, Burl Harris, and Joe Krouse—were elected.

## New Beginnings

On October 15, 1992, the Gascosage Board of Directors announced the hiring of John Greenlee of Wilton, Iowa, as its new general manager. Born in Kansas City and raised in Minnesota, John had a bachelor's degree in business from Kansas State Teachers College in Emporia, Kansas, and came with twenty-two years of experience in the electric cooperative program and utility management. Before coming to Gascosage, John was the assistant general manager for East River Electric Power Co-op, division manager of accounting for Eastern Iowa Light and Power Co-op, and for a time worked as a field accountant for the REA. With a well-qualified manager at the helm, and a few key issues resolved, it was time for Gascosage to put the struggles of the previous few years behind them and face the future. Conflicts, like everything else, have a life span and this one was coming to an end. Walt Weider summed it up well. "Through all the good and the bad," he said, "we have a very strong and positive co-op and that's mainly because of the dedication of our employees."

Working the lines with a hot stick.

Karl Brandt works from the bucket with Craig Rivera on the pole as they hang a regulator.

Upon his arrival, John's first priority was to talk with each of the employees individually in order to assess the tasks at hand. As a result of those conversations, John began working with the board to assemble a policy manual that set detailed standards for employee compensation, board policies regarding the consumers, and other issues. He also instituted a safety program for accreditation and conducted building and equipment inspections. When outages occurred, John went out with the linemen and as a result, stepped up the right-of-way program and changing out poles. An inspection conducted by the Rural Utilities Service (RUS) nearly resulted in a stop order on all future advances of loans, but John was able to put together a plant rehabilitation policy for which RUS approved a loan and which the co-op's insurer also approved. The policies John developed with the board over the next year and a half remain in place eighteen years later.

## Legislative Challenges

With all the other factors driving up the cost of energy, Gascosage, like energy providers across the country, was facing a legislative onslaught that began with the passage of the Clean Air Act in 1990. Power plant smoke stack emissions were to meet government guidelines starting in 1995 and the cost of modifications to power plants to meet these guidelines was projected in the hundreds of millions of dollars.

Despite moves to cap cost increases in such areas as pension benefits and right-of-way clearing, Gascosage suffered an operating loss of about $30,000 in 1992 and the board was considering a rate increase, the first since November of 1984. John Greenlee recalled his second board meeting when he told them, "You don't need a manager as much as you need money to operate." Wholesale power costs were increasing, a result of complying with clean air regulations, and Gascosage was anticipating the need for purchasing new vehicles and line trucks.

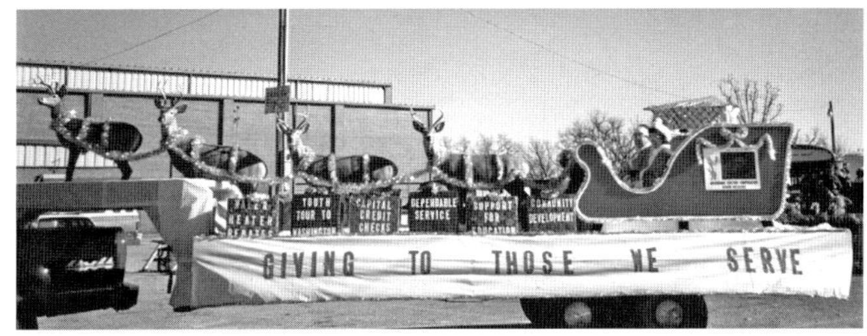

John and Wilma Greenlee play Santa and Mrs. Claus on Gascosage's float in the 1993 Christmas Parade.

Inflation for the period of 1985 to 1993 was 30.24 percent for everything from basic materials to insurance. As a result, Gascosage announced the board had approved a rate increase at its December 1992 meeting, though they still boasted the lowest rates among the surrounding rural electric cooperatives. In a pleasant turn of events, however, the board voted the following June to refund $93,073.78 in capital credits to its members. The first refund in over twenty years, it represented retirement of the 1961 fiscal year and, to their delight, members who were patrons in 1961 received their check at the September annual meeting.

Linemen use a dummy to practice a pole top rescue.

Regulators adjust the voltage on the line to increase the system's efficiency.

In 1994, $700,000 worth of system upgrades to three-phase service were made on nearly ten miles of line in the Iberia area. Said John Greenlee, "This will provide for increased electric requirements of existing consumers and requirements for new consumers. Our engineers have indicated that without these changes the Cooperative would experience voltage problems on several lines in a few years from now." In the Doolittle-Newburg area, approximately 2.5 miles were converted to a larger line. Plans were also made to replace three hundred poles throughout the area that were found faulty during inspection as part of Gascosage's preventive maintenance program to prevent accidents and reduce future outages. Despite the cost of these upgrades, Gascosage was once again able in 1994 to issue capital credits totaling $237,156 retiring fiscal years 1962 and 1963. ■

Linemen raise the flag at the Gascosage headquarters in Dixon

CHAPTER SEVEN

# Serving the Gascosage Community

■ The mid-1990s was a time of relative calm and prosperity for Gascosage. System upgrades were in place, rates were being held steady, and capital credits were being issued. It was time, then, for Gascosage to play an even larger role in improving the quality of life throughout the community.

Back in 1964 Gascosage began selecting four area students—one each from Dixon, Crocker, Iberia, and Newburg schools—to the annual Rural Electric Youth Tour in Washington, D.C. The students had an opportunity to visit national monuments, visit with legislators, and hear speakers on topics related to the rural electric cooperatives. Though Gascosage ceased participating in the program after 1969, they resumed it once again in 1987 and continue to the present day.

Gascosage began offering scholarships for local students in 1994. Named for the co-op's long-standing manager, Luther Riddle, the program was designed to aid students whose parents or guardians were members of the cooperative and who wished to continue their education by attending college, technical college, or trade school. Jean Prater organized the project. The judges for those first scholarships in 1994 included Frank Stork, general manager of AMEC in Jefferson City; Don Wood, director of marketing and member services for AMEC; Jim Jura, general manager of Associated Electric Cooperative, Inc., based in Springfield, Missouri; and Linda Howard, secretary to the manager of administrative services at Sho-Me Power Electric Cooperative in Marshfield, Missouri. The first two years Gascosage Electric Cooperative funded two $500 scholarships.

Winners of the 1995 Youth Tour to Washington, D.C., were Lisa Kennedy of Dixon, Eric Prater of Iberia, Holli Ringer of Crocker, and Karen Smith of Newburg.

From 1996 to 2002 the cooperative awarded ten $500 scholarships; in 2003, eighteen $500 scholarships were awarded; and every year from 2004 to the present eighteen deserving students have received $1,000 scholarships. Three judges now review the scholarship applications—one from AMEC in Jefferson City, one from Sho-Me Power Electric in Marshfield, and one from Associated Electric Cooperative in Springfield. This year, 2011, a representative from the Missouri Electric Cooperatives Employees' Credit Union in Jefferson City filled in when Associated was unable to participate.

In February of 1995, Gascosage installed twenty-nine new streetlights in downtown Dixon at no cost to the city, replacing the old mercury vapor light fixtures with new, high-pressure sodium lights. The new lights provided twice as much light without increasing the city's energy costs making life safer for both drivers and pedestrians.

For the third consecutive year, the board decided at their June 1995 meeting to distribute capital credit refund checks once again, retiring the years 1964 through 1967. The total amount refunded was over $307,000.

Gascosage Electric Cooperative celebrated its fiftieth anniversary at the October 11, 1995, annual meeting. Now boasting 7,423 members and 1,231 miles of line, the cooperative had $9 million in assets with 70 percent equity for their members, far higher than the 40 percent average. Said Manager John Greenlee, "Though it sounds like a lot of money, the Cooperative uses much of

TOP: Gascosage employees at the 1998 annual meeting. Front: Travis Martin, Billy Null, Bob Hathaway, Jim Clark, Shawn Lipscomb, Travis Hauck, and Larry Prater. Standing: Bill Medlen, Ray Howser, Mike Allen, Karl Brandt, Tony Martin, Wilford Alexander, Jason Wilson, Craig Rivera, Bill Thompson, and Dwight Humphrey.

TOP LEFT: Manager John Greenlee, speaker O. B. Clark, Frank Stork from AMEC, and Karl Zobrist, former chair of the Missouri Public Service Commission, at the 1997 annual meeting.

ABOVE: Shown here in 1996, Dixon ambulance personnel provide blood pressure checks and first aid at the Gascosage annual meeting.

LEFT: 1996 Gascosage Board of Directors. Front: Walt Weider, Norma Riddle, and Dean Baker. Middle row: Bill Davis and Joe Krouse. Top: Larry Anderson, Jim Humphrey, Manager John Greenlee, Norman Porter, and Burl Harris.

it, putting it back into the company and the communities it serves. For example, in the last couple of years there have been more than 500 bad poles replaced, several miles of new line strung, new maintenance trucks purchased, a new driveway installed, and several new employees hired. These have all strengthened Gascosage."

What made Gascosage stand out was the employees' collective and individual commitment to their communities. "Some of the people who work for us serve on city and/or school boards, VFW posts, chambers of Commerce, Lion's Clubs and so on," John said. "The Co-op provides free installation and removal of all Christmas decorations, banners for Dixon Cow Days, Bluegrass Festivals, Labor Day celebrations, fall festivals and just about every other event within our communities."

## Keeping a Watchful Eye Out

Perhaps because they were all too aware of the hazards inherent in storms, Gascosage decided to team up with three other cooperatives to provide the people in their areas with an early warning system for severe weather conditions and other emergencies. Along with Howell-Oregon Co-op in West Plains, Crawford Co-op in Bourbon, and Intercounty Co-op in Licking, Gascosage helped donate nearly $103,000 to purchase two weather transmitters. The two transmitters were installed on towers at Bourbon and Summersville in late January of 1996 and were dedicated the following March. In attendance were the managers of the four co-ops plus Richard Augulis, director of the National Weather Service's fourteen-state Central Region; Stan Johnson, program manager for NOAA Weather Radio; Jerry Uhlmann, director of the State Emergency Management Agency; and Don Wood, director of marketing and member services of AMEC. Bob Priddy of MissouriNet served as moderator of the event. Vice President Al Gore, whose initiative to help the National Oceanic and Atmospheric Association expand its Weather Radio Network prompted the project, sent a letter to Crawford's manager Larry Austin saying, "We can all now hope that your association's efforts inspire others around the country to pursue similar projects."

Participating in the 2003 dedication of the weather transmitter are Manager John Greenlee, SEMA Director Jerry Uhlmann, State Representative Bill Ransdall, State Representative Blaine Luetkemeyer, Steve Runnels of the National Weather Service, Gascosage Board President Bill Davis, Kevin Hopper of Sho-Me Power, Superintendent of Dixon Schools Barry Morrow, and Jerry Finke of the National Weather Service.

Going one step further, Gascosage helped purchase several hundred seven-band tone alert radios to provide protection to rural Missourians from severe weather and other hazards. Consumers who wished could purchase the monitors at Gascosage's cost of $30 and some were donated to Mark Twain REACT. Area senior citizens centers, nursing centers, and schools also received monitors.

Kevin Hopper of Sho-Me and Gascosage Manager John Greenlee were among those whose remarks were broadcast live over the radio.

## Nothin' But Net

Gascosage Electric Cooperative held its fiftieth annual meeting in October of 1997 and distributed capital credit refund checks totaling $412,644.55 for the years 1970 through 1974. Gascosage employees and Dixon High School seniors served up a free lunch of ham, potato salad, and baked beans and the Bluegrass Five entertained everyone.

Even more exciting than the free lunch, at least to some, was Manager John Greenlee's announcement that Gascosage had formed a new company called Gascosage Technologies, LLC. Norman Herren, superintendent of Dixon's schools, contacted John to discuss the possibility of bringing "distant learning" to area schools. Distant learning would make it possible for teachers to teach specialized subjects simultaneously in multiple classrooms and the Frisco League, a consortium of the Dixon, Crocker, Iberia, and Newburg school systems to which Gascosage provided power, was eager to provide the schools with both the savings and learning opportunities that would result.

At the time, John Greenlee said, "The Internet was just a buzzword—the rural areas knew a little of what it was about. If you wanted to pay $100 to hook up to a local carrier you could get Internet service, but otherwise we were pretty well isolated."

Coincidentally, Sho-Me was looking into the possibility of putting fiber optics on a transmission line to replace the existing microwave system. If the distribution systems like Gascosage would extend the fiber out from the substations into the local area, they could pick up the commercial traffic that would help pay for installing the fiber optics.

The board formed Gascosage Technologies, LLC and registered the new company with the Missouri Public Service Commission as an approved telecommunications provider. They then began working with an Internet provider that was recommended by the Dixon School System. The provider, YHTI or Your Home Town Internet, agreed to cover the entire area even though portions of it would operate at a loss. The two technology companies, Sho-Me and Gascosage, met with the Frisco League to devise a plan for securing funding for the project. Sho-Me agreed to fund a grant writer to help them secure a grant from the federal government. John's early experience working for the federal government in rural electrification paid off at this point. To write the grant, he hired Walter Petty, an acquaintance who had written the rules for grant requests to the RUS and was now retired. "I figured if anybody knew the in's and out's, he did," John said. Another acquaintance, Randy Tyree, was a former lobbyist for NRECA in Washington, D.C. At John's request, Randy contacted legislators and assisted them in delivering the grant to the RUS offices in the Department of Agriculture along with Mr. Petty.

"All the puzzle pieces fell into place," John said. "We arranged for congressional inquiries to check on the grant request's progress. We were the first to receive a distant learning grant in the state of Missouri through the rural electrification program."

In addition to the benefit to area schools, medical facilities, and libraries, Gascosage members benefited both directly and indirectly. Beyond just receiving Internet service, they now had the convenience of conducting their business with the co-op in the Crocker and Iberia City Halls. Gascosage continues to maintain the fiber optic lines and when the technology company sells off its excess bandwidth, profits go back to the cooperative. The Dixon schools received recognition in 1999 for the progress they'd made in their Technology in Education program.

A new substation was installed in 1998 north of Dixon to help lesson the load on the existing station south of Dixon and support the power draws from Gascosage's outermost areas. Sho-Me provided almost $900,000 in funding to help upgrade existing facilities and Gascosage committed around $200,000 to the effort.

## Deregulation

Another topic floated throughout the industry for a number of years that threatened the future of electric cooperatives and came to a head in the late 1990s—deregulation. A bill was introduced in Congress to repeal the Public Utility Hold Company Act. PUHCA, originally passed in 1935, regulated the interstate electric utility holding companies, allowing them to expand only into contiguous states and restricted certain unfair business practices. Those who lobbied in favor of the repeal contended that increased competition could lead to lower energy costs and improve service. Those who opposed it, including the cooperatives, argued that the best way to hold costs was to protect the member-owned cooperatives from being squeezed out by investor-owned, and therefore profit-motivated, utility companies.

Glenn English, CEO of NRECA and featured speaker, greets members at the 1999 annual meeting with Manager John Greenlee.

In May of 1998, Board President Walt Weider and Manager John Greenlee attended the NRECA's 1998 Legislative Conference in Washington, D.C. Nearly forty board members and managers from Missouri met with Senator Kit Bond and Representatives Ike Skelton and JoAnn Emerson, joining over three thousand delegates from across the country at the conference. "Since we represent rural people in rural America," John said, "we do not desire laws imposed upon us that would be designed to fit or benefit the large metropolitan areas or the super large electric users."

Many folks attending the 1999 annual meeting can recall a time when they had lunch sitting on cinder blocks and boards.

Members enjoy a free lunch with long-time friends and neighbors at the 1999 annual meeting.

Several years previously, the Gascosage bylaws had been changed at the recommendation of the NRECA to protect them from potential take-over by investor-owned utilities. The change implemented rules and procedures for evaluating offers, should they arise, and called for a majority vote by the members, calls for appraisals, and provided for other cooperatives to be given the opportunity to submit competing proposals. To date, no national deregulation plan has been adopted.

By the end of 1999, Gascosage had an impressive list of achievements on behalf of their members. There had been no rate increases since 1993 and over the previous six years they'd issued capital credits totaling $1,432,217. Gascosage's outage time remained lower than both state and national averages.

## Gascosage and AmerenUE

In June 1998, the Missouri Public Service Commission approved a territorial agreement between AmerenUE and Gascosage Electric Cooperative designating the boundaries of both power suppliers in portions of Camden, Miller, Maries, Pulaski, and Phelps Counties. The agreement, which was designed to avoid duplication of facilities and minimize disputes between the two power suppliers, became necessary when AmerenUE extended a line over a road that many years ago was established as a Gascosage service area. The duplication of lines created a safety hazard for the linemen who risk working on a line that they believe is a Gascosage line that's been shut down, only to find it's still hot. The agreement took several years to "hammer out," as John Greenlee put it, but laid the foundation for a win/win acquisition of a portion of Ameren territory by Gascosage.

Towards the Lake of the Ozarks in Camden County, two towns named Brumley and Ulman were situated on the outer edges of AmerenUE's territory. Gascosage was approached by AmerenUE to see if they were interested in acquiring the territory. John Greenlee, satisfied the territory wasn't contiguous to another co-op, arranged for a pole-by-pole inventory to determine the state of the equipment and, thus, the territory's value. What they discovered was approximately 1,200 customers in the area were experiencing brownouts because of low voltage, and hundreds of poles would have to be replaced. The transformer, which would have been more suited to Ameren's urban areas, was oversized for Gascosage's requirements as a distribution co-op, and their right-of-way clearing program was virtually nonexistent.

Al Rodger, assistant administrator with the electric program of the RUS; Bill Davis; Wilma Greenlee; and Jake Warren at the 2002 NRECA annual meeting. Mr. Rodger was to have the final sign-off on the loan for the purchase of the Brumley/Ulman territory.

Janet Beck and Larry Merry from AmerenUE with Manager John Greenlee and Gayle Prater, office manager, during the purchase of the Brumley/Ulman territory in 2002.

Gascosage Board Member Gene Meredith and Dean Baker, board vice president, cut the ribbon on the new Brumley Substation with board members, engineers, and staff looking on.

It was time to get down to price. AmerenUE, it turned out, was looking for a purchase price equal to six times the annual revenue, an amount that was approximately six times what John and Gascosage felt it was worth based on the analysis. "I assumed at that point, that it was a dead issue," John said. However, AmerenUE submitted a counter-offer that was very close to the optimum figure the Gascosage Board of Directors had set and instead of being a "dead issue," on June 21, 2002, the acquisition became a "done deal."

The next step was to secure financing and a loan application was submitted to RUS. Though they indicated acquisitions of this nature were likely to become a trend, this was the first loan made under the RUS for that purpose in a very long time. The total loan was for $3 million, however, none of the funds beyond the purchase price of $1.5 million were used. The rehabilitation of the system was all done through the cooperative's general funds.

In all, the purchase took several years from beginning to end and lots of details had to be worked through. Sho-Me agreed to install a new substation with a new transformer, meters had to be transferred, and the Public Service Commission required the two companies hold joint meetings with both Gascosage members and AmerenUE customers. Gayle Prater was Gascosage's office manager at the time and said, "Their customers had never been part of a co-op so we had to explain the idea of being a member and owner of the Co-op." The ribbon cutting ceremony for the Brumley Substation was held September 14, 2004, making the transfer from AmerenUE to Gascosage Electric Co-op complete.

**REA = RUS**

■ The Department of Agriculture Reorganization Act of 1994 expanded the REA's service to include the building of infrastructure, like water and sewer service, in order to stimulate economic development in rural areas. In April of 1995 the REA changed its name to the Rural Utilities Service.

---

## People Helping People Since 1945

Gascosage's slogan, "People Helping People Since 1945," extended far beyond its usual territory when Hurricane Katrina hit the coastal shore on August 29, 2005. A four-man crew from Gascosage went to the portions of Mississippi hardest hit by the hurricane. No sooner had they returned than Hurricane Rita hit the next month and, again, Gascosage crews went to help out. Four-man crews stayed in the tent city erected by the Federal Emergency Management Association at Lake Charles for two weeks, working around the clock until another four-man crew arrived to replace them. Karl Brandt, who started work at Gascosage in 1974 and has been operations manager since 1995, was among the crews. "The whole area was flooded," Karl said. "We had to work off the edge of the road, trying to stay ahead of the crews setting the poles."

Gascosage linemen donated their time to install new lights at the Crocker High School ballfield.

Under the auspices of the NRECA International Foundation, Gascosage has sponsored Karl on several trips to other countries as well. In 2001, he was part of a team of six men from all over the United States who went to the Dominican Republic to help a village that had been devastated by Hurricane George in 1998. In 2008 he went to a village in Sudan that had been destroyed after twenty years of civil war. Mike Allen joined Karl on a 2009 trip to Bolivia where they trained local crews whose main objective was to get electricity to the water wells for irrigation and drinking water. They spent the first week in the foothills around LaPaz where the elevation was so high it made breathing difficult. The second week they worked in the rain forest where the humidity was so high and termites were so bad they had to use concrete poles. Though they missed having Thanksgiving with their families, both were profoundly moved by the experience. When the well was turned on "the villagers brought us flowers and food—they were so grateful," Mike said. Karl described it as " the biggest day in the villagers' lives."

## A Helping Hand

Sometimes the people of Gascosage help out in small ways that mean everything to the people around them. Sometimes the help is just another day's work, like when a group of linemen donated their time rebuilding the lighting for the Crocker School's ballfield. Other times, it's a bit more dramatic. For example, there was the time lineman Tony Martin was on a pole in Highway D when he heard a man calling for help. Tony found the man had accidentally severed a portion of his hand. He administered first aid and contacted an emergency team from his two-way radio.

On another occasion, a crew was called in after hours in response to a power outage out near Highway 133 and BB. It was a very foggy night and as the men started evaluating the downed power lines, they heard a car horn honking somewhere down in a field. They investigated and found the badly injured person stuck in the car following a wreck. The crew quickly called an ambulance.

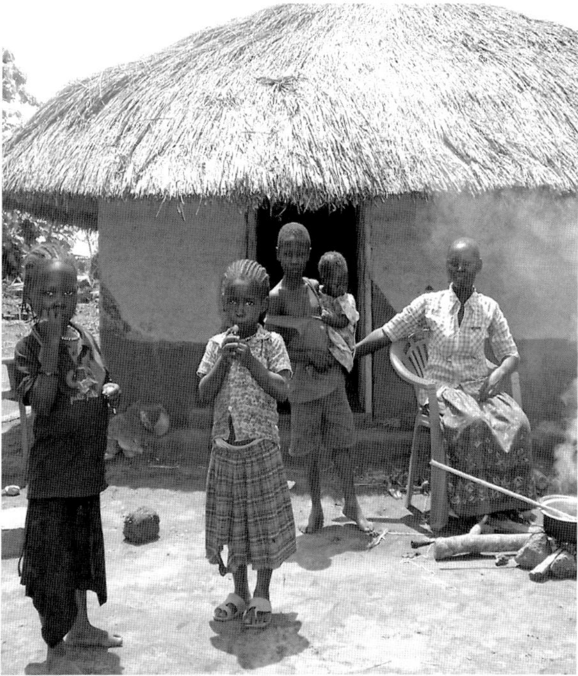

Karl Brandt went to the Sudan in 2008 with NRECA's International Foundation. "I wish everyone could make a trip like this," Karl said. "It would do the whole world good to see how others live—we're the lucky ones."

## Energy and the Environment

The days when cooperatives' biggest concern was getting lines built had come to a close. By 2000, sixty-five years since President Roosevelt signed the legislation creating the Rural Electrification Act, the issues surrounding electrical energy focused less on its generation and distribution and more on its impact on the environment. The phrase "global warming" made its way into the worldwide consciousness as energy and the environment became a politically charged issue.

In front are the 2001 Youth Tour winners: Chris Martin, Meggan Sexton, Julie Rowden and Derek Kelly. Standing with them are Representative Bill Ransdall, Board President Bill Davis, Representative Bob May, Representative Blaine Luetkemeyer, and Senator Sarah Steelman.

Because of inflation and environmental issues surrounding Missouri's high sulfur coal, Associated Electric Cooperative, who owned the mines, was forced to exit the coal business in Missouri and start using western coal from Wyoming to generate power and still comply with the Clean Air Act of 1970. Between 1994 and 2003, Associated cut sulfur dioxide emissions

Gascosage outside employees line up at the 2001 annual meeting. Left to right: Billy Null, Robbie Yoakum, Wilford Alexander, Tony Martin, Shawn Lipscomb, Bill Medlen, Larry Prater, Jason Wilson, Brent Holtsclaw, Mike Allen, Ray Howser, Jim Clark, Bob Hathaway, Dwight Humphrey, and Operations Manager Karl Brandt.

from its entire system by about 90 percent by converting coal units to burn 100 percent low sulfur coal. Sulfur dioxide emissions dropped from 395,204 tons a year prior to the coal conversion to an average of 38,000 tons a year after. Associated also took an aggressive approach at its New Madrid Power Plant to reduce its emissions of nitrogen oxides by installing selective catalytic reduction (SCR) equipment to remove nitrogen oxides. Between 2000 and 2003, Associated added SCRs to both of its coal generating units at New Madrid at a capital cost of more than $100 million and an annual operating and maintenance cost of about $6 million.

Despite environmental concerns, demand for electricity remained on the rise. The Annual Energy Outlook released by the Energy Information Administration in 2004 showed that residential energy use was projected to increase 25 percent by 2025. The future of rural electric cooperatives across the country will be determined by their ability to continue providing affordable electricity while addressing environmental concerns and the resulting legislation and regulations.

Between 2005 and 2008, electric bills across the country increased an average of 30 percent, largely because of increased environmental regulations and rising costs for coal, natural gas, and construction materials. Consumers in the coal-reliant Midwest were expected to experience a larger cost impact from the proposed carbon dioxide regulations.

Gascosage joined the "Our Future, Our Energy" campaign led by the NRECA. Over 700,000 letters, emails, and postcards were sent from Missouri to members of Congress voicing their concerns over the price of electricity in the wake of cap-and-trade legislation. ■

## The Cost of Vandalism

■ According to maintenance crew member Mike Allen, would-be sharpshooters using insulators as targets are the source of a lot of Gascosage headaches. But the worst example of senseless vandalism occurred in February of 2000. Vandals shot an insulator on the Sho-Me Power Cooperative's 161,000-volt transmission line destroying six miles of transmission line and a substation transformer, resulting in outages throughout the region and as far away as Springfield and Kansas City. The new 255,114-pound substation transformer was delivered to Frank's Switch Substation near Dixon via a specially designed railcar. The train was halted for over two hours while contractors maneuvered three 60-ton cranes and a side boom caterpillar to unload it to a 54-ton, 12-axle trailer. The cost for the transformer and delivery was $1.3 million plus another $100,000 for installation and $700,000 to reconstruct the transmission line.

The new transformer making its way to the Frank's Switch Substation.

Crews worked from boats to repair damage when rains from Hurricane Ike caused flooding in the Gascosage area in 2008.

CHAPTER EIGHT

# Protecting a Legacy, Forging a Future

■ Sixty-six years after its incorporation, Gascosage Electric Cooperative serves almost 10,000 members in parts of 5 counties and boasts almost 30,000 poles bearing 1,549 miles of line averaging 6.6 meters per mile. The 2010 member satisfaction report showed Gascosage retains strong support with a customer satisfaction index of eighty-one while the industry average is seventy-five. There is no question both the members and the workers of Gascosage have changed over the years but change, like beauty, is judged in the eyes of the beholder.

Many of Gascosage's current members moved into the area seeking the peaceful life of the Ozark Plateau, and Fort Leonard Wood has brought folks into and out of the area since it was built in 1941. But perhaps more than for anyone else, the years have brought many changes for the linemen. They all serve an apprenticeship now and have to pass a journeyman test. On-the-job training is supplemented with annual classes at AMEC in Jefferson City and some attend Northwest Lineman College out of Linn, Missouri.

The Gascosage team, 2008.

For reasons unknown, the horseplay that lightened the workday years ago has become a thing of the past. Bill Davis was known for his antics back in Gascosage's early years, both in the office and the field, and Larry Prater remembers winters when the linemen built a fire where they were working to roast hot dogs. Walnut fights and snowball fights have also gone by the wayside along with dynamite and the infamous "banjo and spoon" for digging holes. A pressure digger, recently purchased to replace the one originally purchased in 1996, drills right through rock making it possible for the linemen to install six to eight poles in one day's time. Even the radios, that at one time vastly improved communication for the linemen, have been replaced by cell phones. With the gratitude and humility of a man who recalls tougher times in America, Gene Allen looks back on the so-called "good old days" without rancor. "I don't begrudge any of my working conditions because that's the way it was then. I'm just so thankful that these boys have better working conditions."

While not quite as technologically advanced as some of the larger cooperatives, Gascosage has other advantages. "We're a small co-op and we don't have any outlying offices. But we can get to anywhere in our system within forty minutes," said Operations Manager Karl Brandt. Their members, however, are as dependent on technology as the rest of world and mere blinks in the service result in calls to the office. When that happens, maintenance crew member Mike Allen says, "The only solution is to get out and walk, climb every pole, check every insulator. It's a lot of man-hours and people don't realize that."

Gascosage's 2008 Board of Directors: Dean Baker, Gene Meredith, Joe Krouse, Burl Harris, Norma Riddle, Jim Humphrey, Jake Warren, Bill Davis, and Grover Johnson.

Besides using the Internet service that fiber optic lines installed by Gascosage brought to the area, members can also pay their bills online in their homes and several locations in the area. In 2002 Gascosage implemented an automated meter reading system, a far cry from the days when members were given a rate book for reading their meters and calculating their own bills.

However, many traditions do continue at Gascosage. Pat Williams, who worked the front desk for many years, recalled the Christmas parties held over at the old Legion Hall and helping haul food up from Woody's Restaurant. Now she and other retirees look forward to joining the current employees for the annual get-together. Every year since 1987 Gascosage has sent four area high school juniors to Washington, D.C. For the seventeenth consecutive year, Gascosage helped students continue their education. In 2010, Gascosage awarded eighteen $1,000 scholarships. Every year, crews from Gascosage string Christmas lights for the towns in their service territory, donating both their time and the expense of the electricity to the communities.

Annual meetings still include a free lunch and attendance prizes but now they also include free health screenings and flu shots. The children have fun in inflatable bounces and an eighteen-foot-high slide in a circus-like atmosphere. The meeting still opens with the "Star Spangled Banner," followed by the Pledge of Allegiance and an invocation. At the 2010 annual meeting, Board President Jake Warren announced Gascosage was able to issue $472,022 in capital credits to its membership and reported the co-op was maintaining 65.88 percent equity, compared to the national average of 43 percent.

In contrast to the days of "load building," members are now urged to participate in the "Take Control and Save" campaign, addressing issues surrounding energy efficiency including home energy audits. In future decades, it will be increasingly

TOP: Beginning in 2004, Gascosage began sending four students, one from each school, to the CYCLE (Cooperative Youth Conference and Leadership Experience) at the Association of Missouri Electric Cooperatives in Jefferson City. The 2010 winners were Katie Wilson, Kevin Wesley, Morgan Routh, and Allie Cook.

BOTTOM: Winners of the 2006 Youth Tour were LeAnn Barnes, Kristal Burkit, Kody Farnham, and Nick Reynolds.

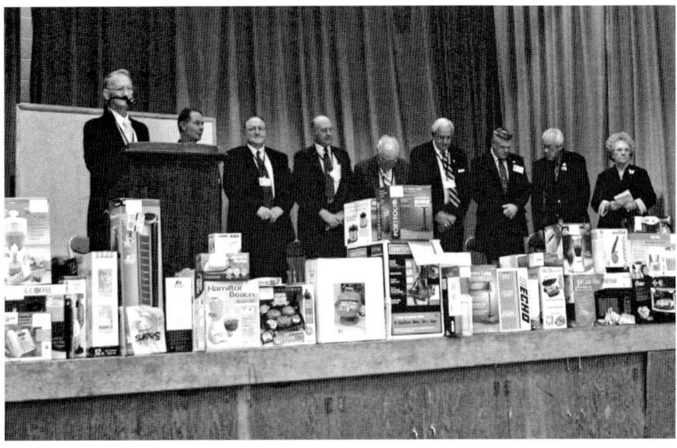

As always, the board members take the stage for the 2010 annual meeting, upstaged by the attendance prizes.

TOP and BOTTOM: Members fill the Dixon High School gymnasium at the 2010 annual meeting.

TOP and BOTTOM: Buddy Bear entertains the children.

Ken Roberts, a local Elvis impersonator, entertained the crowd.

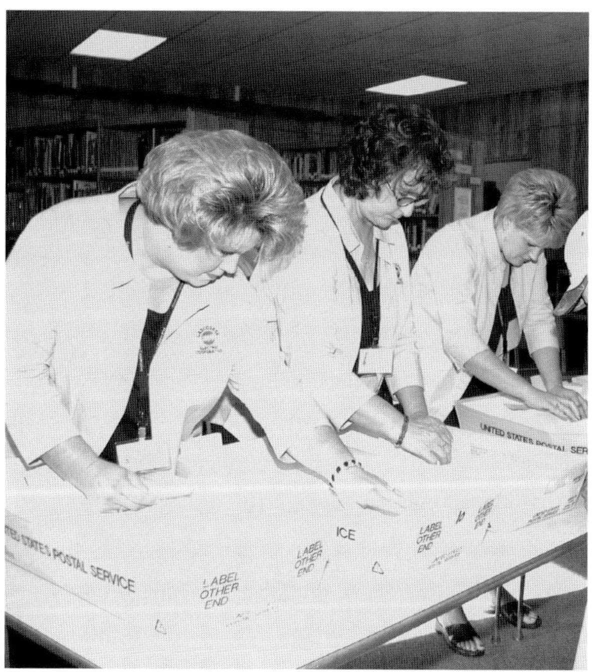


Kim Doyle, Debbie Alexander, and Stacey McKinnon hand out capital credit checks at the 2010 annual meeting.

important for the cooperatives and their members to work together to offset the increasing costs of complying with clean air legislation. In the last six years, Gascosage's wholesale power costs from Associated Electric Cooperative, Inc., have increased 37 percent as a direct result of clean air legislation and its impact on the cost of generating power.

In October of 2003, Gascosage Electric Cooperative held its first annual Grassroots Appreciation Dinner at the Dixon Senior Citizens Center, a facility in which both Luther Riddle and Jean Prater played an instrumental role in founding. Grassroots is a small group of members who keep a watchful eye on legislation impacting the cooperative and work with legislators to help protect it, ensuring that the rural electric consumers' voices are heard. Luther Riddle's words of so many years ago ring true now more than ever: "The members have to be concerned and take an active interest in the Cooperative. The Cooperative must be run for the good of the people."

## The Storm of the Century

The 1987 ice storm was eclipsed in January of 2007 when a storm dubbed "the ice storm of the century" hit the Gascosage area. Ironically, Gascosage had held a meeting just the month before, required by the RUS, to discuss the effective use of manpower, the logistics needed to support them, and to conduct a mock exercise of their emergency restoration plan.

The rain started around 2 p.m. on Sunday, January 14, 2007, and by 6 p.m., 60 percent of the main three-phase feeders were out. The morning after the storm hit, 20 percent of Gascosage's members were out of power, and before it was over outages hit the unprecedented 60 percent level. "By then," John Greenlee said, "we knew we had a problem we couldn't solve by ourselves." The hardest hit areas were Iberia and Crocker where a two-mile-long three-phase line was down and Swedeborg where 2.5 miles of line were down. "Poles snapped like toothpicks," John said, "as electric lines became as big as soda cans" from accumulating ice. Most of the linemen worked three days straight before they could go home. Some took shelter with family whose power was back on and people in the community pitched in preparing food at local churches and schools.

On Sunday, John Greenlee contacted Sho-Me Power and the Missouri Association of Electrical

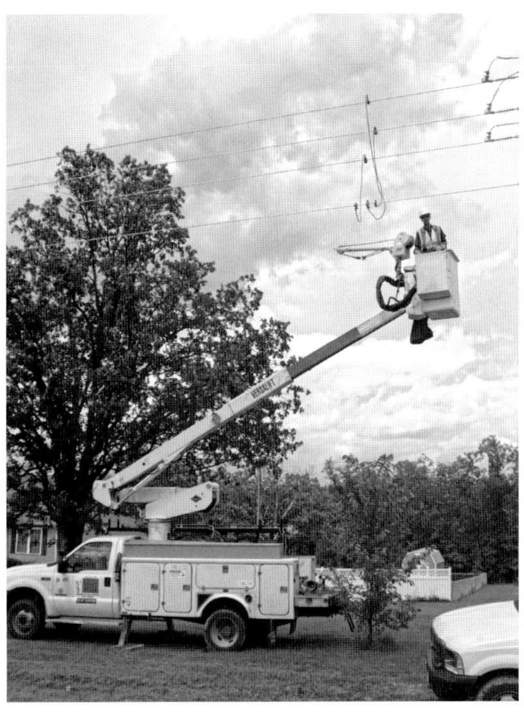

In 2010, lines along Highway BB serving the area northwest of Dixon were converted to three-phase service, providing consumers with three times the current they previously had.

Lovely to look at but treacherous to work in, the 2007 ice storm was dubbed the Ice Storm of the Century.

John Greenlee's helicopter ride revealed downed lines in remote areas.

In 2008, crews from Sho-Me Power and Gascosage Electric worked together rebuilding the Iberia Substation.

Cooperatives asking for help. But with fifteen cooperatives across the state impacted by the storm, no more help was available and by 6 p.m. on Sunday, all the work they'd done to restore power was lost. Mike Allen recalled being at the school at Iberia the day after the storm: "We were at the school eating some soup and the lights started blinking. Somebody called in and said the poles had started falling down and it just went from bad to worse."

John Trapp and Roger Schlichting of Citizens' Electric in St. Genevieve relieved Operations Manager Karl Brandt during the ice storm.

John Greenlee recalled, "We couldn't figure out why we were getting some lines up but it still wasn't working." On Monday, John asked Sho-Me Power to locate a helicopter and a ride over the area revealed lines were down in areas that were too far from the road to be seen. Though they had sufficient manpower from out-of-state co-ops, they were in desperate need of trucks. Again, John called on his friend Larry Merry at AmerenUE for a list of suppliers. But when all he got from the suppliers was the run-around, a call to former representative Bill Ransdall, who was heading up emergency management for Pulaski County, got the equipment on the road the next morning. "Whatever he said," John recalled, "was enough juice to get us the equipment."

Luckily there were only two injuries. Lineman Jimmy Vineyard took a bad fall from a pole when the weight of water and ice proved to be too much. Larry Prater collapsed from exhaustion and was taken to the hospital. "He hadn't eaten anything but candy bars and snacks for three days," his wife Gayle recalled. "I think the guys realized then, they couldn't do that. They needed to go home." After that, the linemen were limited to sixteen-hour shifts.

It took two years to completely clean up after the storm. Twelve of Gascosage's linemen walked 1,500 miles of line over a four-week period making note of problems in preparation for their application for a FEMA grant for 75 percent of the nearly $3.5 million in damages. As a result of their outstanding efforts, the people of Gascosage were acknowledged with a resolution from the Missouri House of Representatives. "Now, therefore, be it resolved," it read, "that we, the members of the Missouri House of Representatives, Ninety-fourth General Assembly, join unanimously to applaud the knowledge, training, skills, and dedication embodied in the work of Gascosage Electric Cooperative Employees members and to convey to all of those involved this legislative body's most heartfelt congratulations for their success in restoring electrical power after severe weather in the state of Missouri during 2007."

Those who recall Gascosage's early days, remember a time when every workday meant that someone's life and livelihood was improved by what they'd done that day. Farm life became easier and more productive, families had more leisure time together and enjoyed the comfort and safety that electricity brought to their homes. The men and women of Gascosage knew their work meant more than stringing lines and recording payments—it was about changing the lives of the rural folks who were their neighbors. Ironically, today we run the risk of taking the electricity on which we have become more dependent than ever for granted.

No doubt those early incorporators would be proud of the job the board of directors, the managers, and the employees have done over the years to provide the members of Gascosage Electric Cooperative with reliable service at the lowest possible cost. They have lived up to their own motto, "People Helping People Since 1945." ■

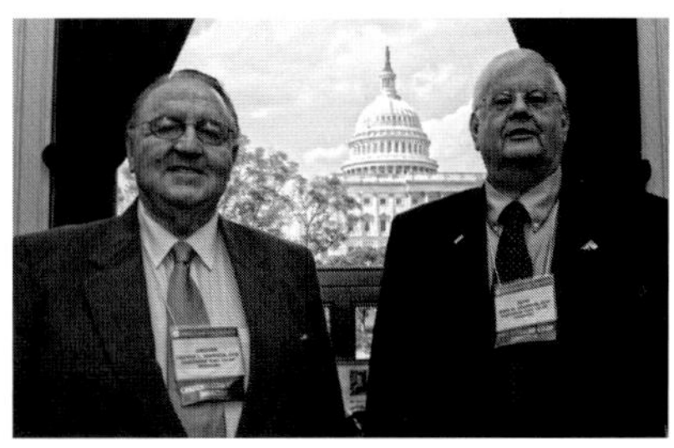

Director Grover Johnson and Manager John Greenlee at the 2009 NRECA Legislative Conference.

Directors Burl Harris and Joe Krouse attended the 2010 NRECA Legislative Conference.

U.S. Representative Ike Skelton met with Gascosage directors during the 2010 NRECA Legislative Conference.

AMEC Manager Berry Hart, U.S. Representative JoAnn Emerson, M&A Electric Power Director Clyde Hawes, Gascosage Director Burl Harris, and Duane Highly of Associated Electric at the 2010 NRECA Legislative Conference.

# Index

# About the Author

■ Pat Swinger began writing for the Donning Company Publishers after working with them to publish her hometown's history during its sesquicentennial in 2006. Pat raised her family in a suburb of St. Louis, during which time she received her degree from Washington University in St. Louis, and then returned to her hometown of O'Fallon, Missouri, in 1996. Since then she has been deeply involved in preserving local history, writing numerous newspaper articles and missives. Because of her abiding passion for local history, she enjoys working with organizations and corporations, helping them to preserve and tell their own stories. ■

Register
can put your Confidence in